Collected Masonic Papers

2020 Transactions
of the
Louisiana Lodge of Research

Collected Masonic Papers

2020 Transactions of the
Louisiana Lodge of Research

MW. Clayton J. Borne, III, 33°, PGM
Worshipful Master
W. Michael R. Poll, PM
Secretary

Published by the Louisiana Lodge of Research
by agreement with
Cornerstone Book Publishers
Copyright as a collection © 2020 by Louisiana Lodge of Research

ISBN: 978-1-61342-362-2

Cornerstone Book Publishers
New Orleans, LA
www.cornerstonepublishers.com

MADE IN THE USA

Table of Contents

Past Masters of the Louisiana Lodge of Research

1989-90: William J. Mollere
1991: Ballard L. Smith
1992: Irving I. Berglass
1993: Philip J. Walker, Jr
1994: Beryl C. Franklin
1995: Ernest C. Belmont, Jr
1996: Thomas P. Brown
1997: Larry H. Moore
1998: Darrell L. Aldridge
1999: Edward W. Brabham, Jr
2000: Howard F. Entwistle, Jr
2001: Johnnie K. Hill
2002: Richard L. James
2003: Terrell Howes
2004: Glenn Cupit
2005: Robert Bazzell
2006: John Bellanger
2007: Jimmy Leger
2008: Ion Lazar
2009: Bill Richards
2010: Ricks Bowles
2011-20: Clayton J. Borne, III

Collected Masonic Papers

Foreword

The preamble to the By Laws of your Louisiana Lodge of Research reads as follows: "The Louisiana Lodge of Research shall be a subordinate body recognized by the Most Worshipful Grand Lodge of the State of Louisiana, F.&A.M. with the object of furthering the genuine principles of Freemasonry, promoting original Masonic research, encouraging, conducting and fostering the study of Masonic topics and diffusing knowledge of Freemasonry's intent and purposes and thereby educating all who come in contact with Freemasonry to be favorably disposed toward Freemasonry's customs, traditions and landmarks."

We can be proud of the accomplishments of our Research Lodge as it has over the past several years accomplishing the objective for which it was chartered, August 15, 1989, by publishing several dynamic Research Sources of old public domain publications along with Books of Transactions. These Books are reflections of the dedicated Research of our Brothers who have submitted papers worthy of publication. This effort has garnered the respect of several National and International organizations and Lodges, some of which have actually applied for membership.

I am most happy that some of our research papers have come from our younger Brothers upon which the future of our Fraternity can rely on long after we have finished our labors in this reality.

I encourage each of you to continue your Research, promote your efforts by presenting and speaking of your Research at your Lodge, because in the end your advancement into light, what you receive from our Order will be in direct proportion to the effort you put into its labors. I encourage those Brothers that have yet to join to become members of our dynamic Louisiana Lodge of Research.

Clayton J. "Chip" Borne, III, WM, PGM

Historical Predicates for Freemasonry in Louisiana

By Clayton J. "Chip" Borne, III, PGM

You are about to journey into, in this Author's opinion, America's ultimate mystique, the "City of New Orleans" and its dynamic "Gumbo" history. It is a place where its eclectic diversity has co-mingled so many years that its identity has matured into something entirely new. The events of the City's history have transformed and molded not only our State but also our Nation. Its "Creole identity" has had a dramatic effect on that history and the "History of Freemasonry" especially its Scottish Rite footprint in Louisiana. Napoleon Bonaparte, although never stepping foot in Louisiana, becomes a Major Character in its development. His older brother, Prince Joseph Bonaparte, was a Mason and was appointed Grand Master of the Grand Orient of France. His Deputy was Jean-Jacque-Regis Cambaceries, also a Freemason and Lawyer who developed for the Emperor, the Napoleonic Code of Civil Laws based on the Ancient Justinian Roman Codes. The history was a French endeavor which would in its development influence all social, political, legal and fraternal identities in Louisiana for many years. Our mystical adventure begins with the chronological review of the people and historical events as predicates to this research project.

In 12,000 BC, the "Prehistoric Era" in Louisiana begins with the first inhabitants and concludes with the arrival of the Europeans. The earliest inhabitants of Louisiana were the Paleo Indians who were nomads constantly in search of food and shelter. They were followed by the Meso Indians (6,000 BC) who banded into larger groups and became less mobile. They were known for their mound building, such as Poverty Point, which culture spanned from 2,000 BC to 600 BC. It is located in northeast Louisiana with communities found in Mississippi and

2

Alabama. They were followed by Tchefuncte Culture, 600 BC to 200 AD. They were followed by the Marksville Culture who organized community life, and just as in Freemasonry, instructed craftsmen and officiated at burial ceremonies at their burial mounds. They were followed by the Troyville-Coles-Green Culture who developed methods for cultivation of crops. They were followed by the Caddo Culture in northwest Louisiana. They developed utilitarian pottery from 1100 AD to 1400 AD. By the time Europeans reached Caddo villages in the 1500s, they were divided into groups or tribes. They supplied the Europeans with salt, furs, horses and food in exchange for beads, guns, knives, etc. The contact with Spanish and French explorers ended the Prehistoric Era forever changing the inhabitant's life and culture.

In 1539, Hernando de Soto, a Spaniard, who, after explorations to the West Indies, and Peru sets out on an Expedition to North American. Landing in what is now Florida, crossing what will become Georgia and Alabama and continuing west he discovered the Mississippi River. De Soto became, the First European Explorer to traverse the mighty waterway. The Mississippi River will become a wide muddy superhighway of activity that will be the catalyst for much of the development of Louisiana.

In 1682, we continue our story with French Explorers, Rene' Robert Cavelier, and Sieur de La Salle who set out on an Expedition to explore the mighty Mississippi River from Canada to the Gulf of Mexico. The Expedition would give France an international claim over the river and lands which would become known as the Louisiana Purchase. That claim was to include the entire territory drained by the river's waterway which encompasses the present states of Louisiana, Mississippi, Arkansas, Missouri, Illinois, Iowa, Wisconsin and Minnesota. All of this vastness he gathered under a single name which was a tribute to King Louis XIV, "Louisiana."

In 1714, Natchitoches, a French Fort and trading settlement was established on the Red River by a French

3

Canadian, Louis Antoine J. de St. Denis, as the first known permanent European settlement in what was to become the Louisiana Purchase. In England, Queen Ann's War had ended with George I of the House of Hanover becoming King marking the beginning of England's Supremacy. This status will remain in play until the events in Louisiana, 100 years later, changed the chessboard.

In 1718, Pierre Le Moyne, Sieur D'Iberville and his younger sibling, Jean-Baptiste Le Moyne, Sieur D'Bienville, French explorers, embarked on a mission to establish a settlement near the mouth of the Mississippi River. In opposition to his engineers, who wanted the City established just south of present-day Baton Rouge, it was Bienville who selected the site for what was to become the Heart of New Orleans, the French Quarter.

In 1720, John Law, an aggressive Scotsman managed to wrangle from the King of France, a 25-year charter to develop the Louisiana Territory. Under Law's orders, Bienville founded the settlement named it after Law's best friend, the King's nephew, Philippe, Duc of Orleans, "La Nouvelle Orleans." Law promised 250 eager concessioners who fell for his real estate scam, abundant wealth. Men were the first settlers in 1719. Some women, who also believed Law and followed later the same year. After word got back to France of the raw, unwelcoming nature of the settlement, the migration slowed. Desperate Law, to keep the male population, had females released from Paris's most notorious prisons in exchange for passage to Louisiana. German's were then brought in to teach the struggling populous how to farm and feed themselves.

By 1727, Religious Orders were established in the City with Roman Catholics, Capuchins, Jesuit and Ursuline Religious Identities, enhancing the French culture and education. The Jesuit connection to Freemasonry especially in the 18th Century is most interesting. The population in New Orleans at this time totaled 940 comprised of 796 Caucasians, 127 Black slaves and 17 Indian slaves.

In 1750, Freemasonry in New Orleans was officially confirmed by the *Sharpe Bordeaux Documents* which manuscripts were discovered in Paris in 1926. Also, these documents confirm Freemasonry's presence was actually known to have been established in Louisiana in the 1740's. The identity was connected with the French fur trade on the Mississippi, which economic endeavor was first established by the early La Salle Expedition of 1682. The manuscript evidence further confirms a 1750 petition with a symbolic charter arriving in the City in 1752 which authority established a French Craft Lodge. Thereafter, in 1756, a Scottish Rite "Ecosse" Lodge of Perfection was chartered for New Orleans both bodies chartered out of the Mother Lodge in Bordeaux, France. These Lodges were both named Perfect Harmony. The *Sharp Bordeaux Documents* confirm that by 1756, the complete system for the pure unadulterated Scottish "Ecossia" Rite of Perfection was legally authorized, established and conferred in New Orleans.

In 1763, Europe's Seven Year a/k/a America's French and Indian Year War ended. England received all lands east of the Mississippi except for the Isle of Orleans by virtue of the Treaty of Fountainbleau and later, the Treaty of Paris. France ceded Louisiana, west of the Mississippi to Spain and New Orleans became a Spanish colony. The people of New Orleans didn't know they had come under Spanish domination for four years. When the French population did finally hear the news, they rebelled and expelled the newly arrived Spanish Governor, Antonio Ulloa, which rebellion created for a period of time an independent republic. Because of the Spanish Inquisition, Freemasonry in Louisiana was at risk. Freemasonry in New Orleans became a secret Brotherhood from 1763 to 1793.

In 1769, Don Alexandro "Bloody" O'Reilly arrived in New Orleans, took command as governor, quieting the Rebellion of 1768, executing many of its leaders responsible for expelling governor, Ulloa. The rebellion was orchestrated primarily by confirmed French leaders of the Masonic community, to include but not limited to, Chouriac, Caresse,

Milhet, De Lanlande, Batard, Carlier, Chantalou, de Lafreniere, Rooks, Grandchamps, Jung, Pellerin, Rousillon, Tiphaine, and Villere families. Many of the Patriots were executed by a firing squad, with the remainder captured and imprisoned in Cuba.

The 1776, American Revolution experienced limited engagements with the British in Louisiana. Spain did seize British emplacements in and about the Gulf Coast Region which actions increased Spanish dominance in the Region, including New Orleans. Spain further increases their presence recruiting immigrants from the Canary Island, "Is lenos" to bolster their military presence in an anticipated escalation of the war with England. Jefferson's "Declaration of Independence" was a dynamic statement of human freedom that inspired not only Americans, but people all over the world.

The 1800 Treaty of San Idefonso where in Emperor Napoleon Bonaparte convinced Spain to cede the Louisiana Territory back to France. This, plus, Spanish interference with shipping on the Mississippi, closing the Port of New Orleans to Americans in 1802, so disturbed President Jefferson that he authorized the Secretary of State, James Madison, to dispatched Robert Livingston to Paris to seal a purchase agreement to acquire only New Orleans, the Florida Parishes and Navigation Rights to the Mississippi River. Because of several recent defeats Napoleon had suffered, the Emperor was happy to sell not only the city but the entire Territory to the United States for a mere 15 million dollars. President Thomas Jefferson on the eve of the Louisiana Purchase stated: "There is on the globe one single spot, the possessor of which is our natural and habitual enemy. It is New Orleans, through which the produce of three-eighths of our territory must pass to market".

Napoleon spoke solemnly, "I am fully sensible of the value of Louisiana," he said, "and it was my desire to repair the error of the French diplomatists who abandoned it in 1762 in its transfer to Spain. I have now scarcely received it before I run the risk of losing it; but if I am obliged to give it up, it shall hereafter cost more to those who force me to part with it than those to whom I yield it". The British were forcing Napoleon Bonaparte to part with Louisiana. Great Britain had taken from France, Canada, Cape Breton, Newfoundland, Nova Scotia and the richest portions of Asia. The English were also engaged in exciting troubles in French Santo Domingo. Napoleon would never see Louisiana and the home his loyalist built for him in the French Quarter, the "Napoleon House."

Napoleon then told his ministers what he had assembled then to hear, that to deprive Great Britain of "all prospect of ever possessing Louisiana" he was inclined to cede it to the United States. The next day he brusquely met with Barbe' and Talleyrand instructing them to sell the Louisiana Territory to the United States for not less than "sixty million francs".

Robert R. Livingston, American minister to France, knowing he was authorized just to acquire New Orleans had purchased without authority the entire Louisiana Territory for more money than the United States had in its treasury. Talleyrand said to Livingston and Monroe, "You have made a noble bargain for yourselves", "I trust that you will make the most of it". The purchase agreement had committed the United States to pay France $15 million dollars for what, years later, would be finally counted as almost a billion acres.

Napoleon was resolute in his decision that Great Britain should not have the Mississippi River and of Britain's desire to take possession of it. "It is thus they will begin the war," Napoleon said, referring to the war he knew was coming with Great Britain, for which Napoleon was indeed massing troops in Boulogne for a cross-channel invasion, despite the blockade by Lord Nelson. "The British have 20 vessels in the Gulf of Mexico, and our affairs in Santo Domingo are daily getting worse since the death of General LeClerc." Napoleon felt that he did not have a moment to lose in putting it out of reach."

In 1803, the Louisiana Purchase was perfected at the Cabildo overlooking what is now Place' d Arms. On November 30, the official transfer of Louisiana from Spain to France took place. Less than a month later, on December 20, 1803, at the same location, France passed ownership to the United States. Napoleon's Farewell Statement Foretold the Future, "Let the Louisianans' know that we part from them with regret, recollect that they were Frenchmen and that France, in ceding them has secured for them advantages which they could not have obtained from a European Nation, however paternal it might have been" and "I have just given England, a maritime rival that sooner or later will lay low her pride." Subsequent thereto, Gov. W.C.C. Claiborne began the task of trying to get along with the Creole population and easing out the Spanish officials who seemed unwilling to leave New Orleans. The line dividing the Territory from what was to become the State was the 33° parallel. When Louisiana became a state in 1812 its area was basically what it is today, i.e., defined as "that part of the Louisiana Purchase lying just below the 33° latitude." Even the State's geographical boundaries have Masonic Symbolism. Gov. Claiborne, a member of Perfect Union Lodge F & AM despite the ever-present clash of culture, moved to Americanize the City.

In 1805, the City of New Orleans was officially incorporated as a municipality, legally establishing a city government, with a mission; duties, privileges and boundaries. Two of the most important events in New Orleans history and in fact the history of the United States, are the Louisiana Purchase and the Battle of New Orleans both events orchestrated and perfected in the city assisted by its civil leaders, many of whom were Freemasons. Bernard de Marigny de Mandeville's plantation below the City is subdivided into an area now known as the Bywater District. De Marigny, a prominent Mason, was declared by numerous historians to be the richest man in Louisiana. An avid gambler, he is said to have invented the dice game of "craps." Other dynamic city leaders, developers and

Masons, with names like Sarpy, Duplantier, Saulot, Robing and Livaudais contributed in developing New Orleans. All were prominent Masons.

In 1812, Louisiana becomes a State being admitted into the Union, as the 18th State. The Political boundaries called "Parishes" were established as opposed to the "Counties" as in Common Law States. This was a result of the dominant influences of the Catholic Church in the City. In addition, in the same year the Grand Lodge of Louisiana was constituted by Five French Lodges meeting in the City, all of which were holding York Rite Charters. The inviting founder Perfect Union was joined by Charity, Concord, Perseverance and Etoile Polaire. The chronology of their numbering reflected each lodges receipt of their York Rite Charters. The two English Lodges in the City, Louisiana and Harmony, because of the dominant French Influence of the participating Lodges decided not to initially join.

In 1812, the War with England divided the Citizens of the United States into the distinct factions, namely, New England doves and Southern and Western hawks. It was, in fact, an echoing of the divisiveness that had resulted from the Louisiana Purchase. At the time of Jefferson's land deal, federalists such as Alexander Hamilton thought the addition of more un-surveyed wilderness to the United States would result in ruin. During this time, the New England idea of secession to form a Northern Confederacy had taken root. The reason creating the conflict is not emphasized or even realized by many. The conflict revolved around British interference with American commerce on the High Seas. The citizens of the new nation were clearly not united. The reason for the division was that most American money was in New England banks and New Englanders were doing good business with the British Navy despite the war. The rationale was that they were outfitting British ships for action against Napoleon. In reality, one hundred miles of Maine's coastline was completely in British hands. This issue was reflected in American Freemasonry as the majority of Masonic Lodges in the British Army were warranted under Irish Constitutions, so Masonry in the colonies was predominantly Irish.

In 1815, the Battle of New Orleans was launched by the British as a final attempt to seize the City and put an end to the War that began in 1812. The Battle of New Orleans was in fact a full campaign over four months with eight land and sea engagements. General Andrew Jackson, who was to become Grand Master of the Grand Lodge State of Tennessee and seventh President of the United States, was sent to protect the City. In the last battle of the last war ever fought between the United States and Great Britain, Jackson's eclectic mix of Tennessee volunteers, Kentucky Long rifles, Freemen of Color, Creole French, Germans, Spanish, Choctaw Indians and the Lafitte's Privateer Navy prevailed. The Battle of New Orleans cost the British more than 2,000 men. It cost Jackson 71. In February of that year, the whole country rejoiced in a new nationalism forgetting that six months before the Treasury had been empty, the government powerless to raise an effective army and the Union threatened with opposing political persuasions and threatened dissolution. Three seldom reported, historical events shaped the unifying results of the War.

1) "Northern Confederacy?" As General Jackson was marching down the Natchez Trace with his troops, a meeting was being held in Hartford, Conn., by New England Federalists to discuss "public grievances and concerns" and the possibility of entering into a separate peace with Great Britain by the New England states who were actively attempting to form and entering into an independent Northern Confederacy to be aligned with England as per the authority of and as guided by their own doctrine of "States' Rights".

2) "States' Rights?" Massachusetts and Connecticut actually sent commissioners to Washington to place their protest before Congress however they arrived at the same time as the news of Jackson's overwhelming victory at New Orleans. Whatever they had to say was forgotten. Interestingly, years later, these same Northern States would

object to the use of the "States Rights Doctrine" by the Southern States resulting in the "War against Northern Aggression" or above the Mason Dixon Line the "Civil War".

3) "Pirates?" To the Leadership of the City, they were an unruly aggravation. To the citizens of New Orleans, they were patriot privateers primarily because of their common enemy the British and their quality supply of British goods at bargain prices. Many of the names appearing on the Privateer Navy's manifestos were also listed on the Lodge Rosters of Freemasons. No record has been found to confirm Jeans Laffite, however his brother, Dominique, was an active Mason and is buried in St. Louis Cemetery # 2 in the city. One of the most interesting stories often told by historians was that in 1813 before the Battle of New Orleans, Governor W.C.C. Claiborne issued a $ 500.00 reward for the arrest of privateer, Jean Lafitte. A response came from Captain Lafitte offering $ 1000.00 to anyone who would deliver Governor Claiborne to Barataria. The notice was signed "Jean Lafitte." Following Lafitte's decision to have his privateer Navy fight with the Americans, full pardons were issued for all. The privateers were experienced military and played a major role in the success of the war and its victorious claim for American Independence.

Conclusion: The City of New Orleans' Louisiana Purchase, was center stage which for Thomas Jefferson, represented a defining moment in the history of the United States as it doubled the size of the young nation and insured free and open navigation of the Mississippi River. This was essential for the westward expansion of the Nation. The Louisiana Purchase has been the subject of much literary critiques especially the events involved in the Battle of New Orleans as having no military value because of the signing of the Treaty of Ghent, which Concordant was alleged to have made peace with England. It was signed December 24, 1814, only days before the main engagement in New Orleans. This Author concurs with other Louisiana historians in that, had General Packenham, also, a Brother Mason, commander of the spoiled expedition, deployed his troops as skirmishers instead of marching them head on in line abreast into the concentrated rifle fire of the finest marksmen in the world, who can tell.

The War in New Orleans was essentially a Second War of American Independence. Treaties must be validated by the countries that sign them. If the British were victorious in New Orleans, would the Treaty of Ghent, signed by the British and the American representatives in Ghent, Belgium, ending the War of 1812 been honored by England? Some historians have suggested further that after the Treaty of Paris was signed in 1783, ending the American Revolutionary War, the British had no intention of honoring it. In essence the War of 1812 and its Victory in New Orleans in 1815 defeated England's attempt to reclaim her original thirteen colonies.

The Louisiana Purchase without question altered the course of American History. The History of New Orleans with its English, French, German, African and American Indians historical adventures in the development of Louisiana is romantically intriguing and provocatively tragic. A major portion of those exploits were Freemasons who embraced the Craft and were guided, as we will see, by its moral code of justice. This research has established the foundation for the Development of the Royal Order of Freemasonry and then guide us through that journey in French Louisiana.

References

Fryarre, Charles - *History of Louisiana*, Reprint Gram Co., 1965, Vol. IV, Pg. 58, 122
Core, Jesse: *Understanding the Louisiana Purchase*, (Jan 1983) pg. 71,72,73
Mollere, William J.: *Development of Scottish Rite LA Lodge of Research*, Vol.1
Veland, A., *Marquis De Lafayette*, New Age (1955) pg. 593

Green, Dr. Glenn L.: *Masonry in Louisiana, A Sesquicentennial History 1812-1962*

Grand Lodge, State of Louisiana F&AM *Proceedings,* 1900, 1965, 1977, 1997, 2002, 2009

Carter, James D: *History of the Supreme Council*, Vol. 2&3, 1853, pg. 12-20

Krug, Mark M.: *Rise of the American Nation,* Pg. 140, 230, 237,264

Conrad, Glenn: *Dictionary of Louisiana Biography,* 1998, Vol. 1 & 2

Kemp, John: *New Orleans,* 1981, Windsor Publications, Pg. 31

Conrad, Glenn: *The German Coast,* University of Southwestern Louisiana Publishing, Pg. 17

The Ancient Mystery Schools
By Michael R. Poll

We often hear that Freemasonry is tied to the ancient mystery schools through initiation. But this presents us with several basic and important questions. What were the ancient mystery schools and what is initiation?

Early man lived off the land and hunted for the food that he needed. Groups of humans would gather together for both protection and social interaction. From all that we can gather from available information there was always a realization that there was something more and greater, whose hand guided all actions and creations. There was also the desire to reach out and touch the unknown.

Also, in early records and archaeological evidence we can find traces of humans practicing various ceremonies and initiations. These initiations could be part of a child growing into adult hood, ceremonies following death, or individuals simply seeking something greater out of life. In all cases it is clear that there was a desire to be something more. Why such a desire existed, we don't know. Why there has always been a deep feeling in humans that there *was* something more, we don't know.

We can find many examples of initiation in numerous ancient societies and groups. One of the common threads through all of these examples is that there are, most often, three similar conditions that are required for an initiation to be considered valid. These three conditions are, a desire to initiate, a desire *to be* initiated, and the proper setting.

If we look at a Masonic lodge and examine how we initiate candidates we can find the same three conditions of initiation in practice in our lodges. When a candidate petitions to join Masonry, that is the desire *to be initiated.* He has taken an active step of his own free will. When a lodge ballots on and accepts a petition that is *the desire to initiate.*

The proper setting of a lodge is when an initiation takes place with the membership being respectful of the initiation and void of humor or distracting side discussions.

There is a thought that when one receives a proper initiation, a door is opened for them. But a door to what? The suggestion is that the door leads to another room … a symbolic room of enlightenment, spiritual growth, and wisdom. But initiation itself does not give us these things, it only makes them availabe.

Rosicrucian philosophy speaks of one identified as the Dweller on the Threshold. This individual stands in an open doorway, but he does not enter the next room. He stands outside of the room filled with wonderful things. He does not take advantage of any of it by simply taking the next step of walking into the room.

Initiation is not the end goal for the true Seeker of Light. Initiation only opens the door for us but it is required for us to walk in and use the initiation as a means of advancing ourselves and gaining enlightenment. The responsibility of action is ours.

Wisdom through initiation was often a lifelong process for the initiates in many of the ancient, enlightened cultures. A great center of wisdom was Alexandria, Egypt. Every imaginable area of enlightened study was available to students in Alexandria. Alexandria was located on the main trade routes and the area brought in many seeking greater knowledge of the esoteric arts. The hidden and reserved teachings from around the world were gathered together, studied and preserved in Alexandria.

But there was another important aspect of Alexandria. It was the large complex of libraries.

The libraries of Alexandria are the most famous in antiquity and most likely the largest ever assembled in ancient times. The libraries are said to have contained over a million documents containing the wisdom of the ancient worlds. When these libraries were destroyed, humanity was deprived of more knowledge than we can possibly ever realize.

The destruction of these libraries also sealed off from us the source of the wisdom contained in these libraries. It is very possible that the source of the wisdom contained in these libraries were the libraries themselves. Enlightened initiates may have used these libraries not only as a source of knowledge, but as research centers where theories could be studied and developed. But all that remains today are rumors, stories and fables about the libraries and through them, with them, and because of them, the ancient mystery schools.

It is interesting that it was not until the early 1800s that any serious attempt was made at studying the Egyptian hieroglyphics. This presents us with the obvious question that if so little was known of ancient Egyptian language at the foundation and early days of speculative Freemasonry, then why does so much of our ritual so closely resemble ancient Egyptian ritual? Where did the early speculative Freemasons derived this knowledge? Suggestions that it could be coincidence borders on the irrational. Even the mention of the ancient mystery schools in our Masonic teachings suggest some tie to the schools. And what is the tie? Initiation.

Given the vast amount of what we do not know of our early history, I do not believe that it is that great a leap to suggest that ancient teachings, including those of initiation, traveled down through ancient times, through the Operative Masons and developed into what we know as Speculative Freemasonry.

The ancient mystery schools can be looked at as a collection of formal or informal bodies of esoteric instruction. We can assume that in order to gain admission to one of these *schools* a candidate would need to pass through a rigorous screening and examination into their character. Following an examination into their worthiness they would take part in an initiation or some form of a Rite of Passage.

We can look at so many aspects of our Masonic initiation as well as our Masonic philosophy and teachings, and realize that so much of it is archaic. Our settings, furniture, symbols, words, and practices do seem to come from a different place and time. It is not difficult to see the similarities between our Hiramic legend and the legend of Osiris. It is not difficult to see many ancient teachings, traditions and symbols borrowed by Freemasonry from long-lost civilizations. But who were these civilizations?

Based on new discoveries and research our understanding of ancient Egypt would seem to need complete reexamination and rethought.

Its level of scientific expertise and cultural development appear to be much greater than what is accepted by classical academia. Look at the massive and perplexing Sphinx. It was built during a time when there was not supposed to be any civilization in the area at all. What technology was there in place at the time of the building of the Sphinx? We have no idea.

Look at what we know of early Egyptian language, religion, and philosophy. At the beginning of the old Kingdom and the first pharaohs we see there an *intact hieroglyphic* system, which was their complete writing system. We also see a *complex* science, religion and philosophy. Their whole system seems to have been there at the very beginning of the old Kingdom. How is that possible? How is it possible to begin something as complex as the ancient Egyptian society with everything in place at the very beginning?

Rare and early documents suggest much older advanced civilizations existing long prior to the time of the old Kingdom. Maybe these older civilizations contributed to what would become their language and society. These very ancient and advanced civilizations may have been responsible for the building of many of the wonderful structures attributed to ancient Egypt. Clearly there is so very much that we simply do not know.

But let's now look at the often misunderstood and equally mysterious Rosicrucians. The famous Brotherhood of the Rosy Cross. For the uninitiated, it is said that to try and understand the Rosicrucians is to try and grab handfuls of smoke. While it is sometimes difficult to sort the history from the lore, there are certain aspects of the Rosicrucians that we can look at and study … from a certain perspective.

Rosicrucianism has long been associated with both Freemasonry and the ancient mystery schools. It has been suggested that the Rosicrucians and the Freemasons are something of first cousins. The fact is that trying to understand the early history of the Rosicrucians is as difficult as trying to understand the early history of Freemasonry.

While the history of both orders is obscured and difficult to impossible to completely understand, there is a thread that runs through the philosophy of both Orders that is kindred and somewhat traceable. An old Rosicrucian thought is that either one has always been a Rosicrucian, or they never will be one. While this statement makes no sense from an organizational standpoint, if we look at it from a philosophical view, then it takes on new meaning.

The suggestion would seem to be that it is the Rosicrucian *philosophy*, not the organization, that is at the heart of being a Rosicrucian. One is a Rosicrucian if they embrace its philosophy. Like Freemasonry, the Rosicrucian philosophy seems to have a life of its own separate and apart from the organization.

Also, like Freemasonry, the Rosicrucian Order has a distinct Egyptian flavor to it. Much of its philosophy, rituals, symbols, teachings, and even art is Egyptian in nature. Again, like Freemasonry, the Rosicrucians Order draws an association between itself and a particular medieval order, the Knights Templer. The Rose Croix, the Rosy Cross, the Order Rosae Crucis. All with the same theme, design and suggestion. The Order of the Red Cross. But there is no clear answer *as to why*.

Faint lines… rarely traceable do seem connect these secretive Orders, and for those capable of connecting obscured dots, trace what we have today, through esoteric philosophy, to the early days of man. And what connects them all, is initiation.

In very ancient Egypt, the all-seeing eye was known as the Eye of Horus or the Eye of Ra. Through various myths this was a symbol of healing, protection, and wisdom. The left eye of Horus was said to be the moon and the right eye the sun. Some have suggested that the right and left "all-seeing eyes" reflect the two known decedents of the Ancient Mystery Schools: the Rosicrucians and the Freemasons.

If the suggestion is that the Ancient Mystery Schools, the great temple at Karnack, transformed from a place of esoteric instruction into an active Order with the goal of preserving sacred wisdom and transmitting to it to future generations, then it is not difficult to see a very unscientific and unproven chain of transmission. We can see early Jewish and Christian mystery traditions, including (but hardly limited to) the Nazarenes, the Essenes, the Jacobites, the Templars, the Operative Masons, the Rosicrucians and Speculative Freemasonry. All passing on a secret tradition, a wisdom, a philosophy to future generations of initiates.

It would be naïve to suggest that we have many, if any, real answers. It would seem that we can be likened to a fully grown man with a rich, full history, but one with amnesia. All the details of his life would exist, but they would be unknown to him. But this is only when we examine ancient Egyptian traditions. Ancient Eastern traditions also exist. The Hindus and Buddhists and many others also have rich esoteric traditions.

In India, an ancient Sanskrit text informs us that the Hindu god Shiva has three eyes. One Rosicrucian writer suggests that this third all seeing eye reflects in, Western esoteric tradition, the triad of the Western ancient mystery schools which include the Rosicrucians, the Freemasons, and the Roman Catholic Church. All three have ceremonies of initiation, teach through symbolic lessons, and preserve wisdom to pass on to future generations.

Is any of this theory provable through scientific examination? Not at all. But prove that you love the

Almighty. There are limits as to what can be proven through science, but no limits as to what is acceptable to a belief system. The poet Khalil Gibran once wrote, *"Faith is a knowledge within the heart, beyond the reach of proof."* We must have science to keep us grounded in reality, but if we are to have true balance than we must also have the creative imagination of a child and the courage to believe, even if what we believe cannot be proven through science.

If Freemasonry is only a club for the social enjoyment of our members and if our ceremonies of initiation are only plays designed to entertain and mimic things that we don't understand, then nothing that we do is of any great importance. We might as well entertain ourselves in better ways. Certainly, there are many more ways that we can entertain ourselves that are more satisfying than listening to minutes or arguing over bills.

But if Freemasonry is more than a club than maybe it is worth a closer look. I believe that we are *much* more than a club. I believe that *initiation* is that element within us that not only ties us to the Ancient Mystery Schools, but makes the past as relevant today as it was in ancient times.

It is clear to me that our Masonic initiation, when properly done, opens that mystic or spiritual door for us and gives us the opportunity to explore much deeper aspects of ourselves. It's up to us if we want to walk through that door leading to deeper corners of ourselves, enlighten ourselves, explore ourselves and grow to our limits. No one will force us. In fact, many times only few are aware of exactly what we have in our initiations. They are *themselves* as the Dweller on the Threshold- at best! We must understand that there are times when our leaders and teachers will be woefully ignorant of the treasure that is at our fingertips. It doesn't matter who is at fault for this situation. It simply exists.

There are a few things sadder than seeing the opportunity of initiation wasted because individuals, with no clue as to the true nature of Freemasonry, use our ceremonies as sources of entertainment. The candidate may not be aware that anything has gone wrong, but he will also likely not be aware of that *special something* that many candidates feel when initiation *is* done properly. Placing blame and insulting either the unknowing or the knowing who allowed the levity or distractions is of little benefit. We must see Masonic initiation as a responsibility, an honor and a gift that we have to share.

What we have in Freemasonry is clearly old and it has been clearly important to many people for a very long time. This does not mean that we can prove an actual lineage to anything. If we believe the skeptics, there may be actually nothing of any value in an initiation - no matter if it is done properly or improperly. On the other hand, maybe, it is far more important, far older and far more significant than we have any idea.

I, for one, believe that valid Masonic initiation is one of the keys to a rewarding life. I believe that in all aspects of the lodge, we are to show respect, care and reverence.

Ashlars of the Temple
By Mark St. John

Introduction

We learn that the rough and perfect ashlar are two of the three movable jewels of a Lodge.₆ Stones quarried for structures begin as rough, crude cubes which are then carefully shaped, measured, and checked until they are perfect stones suitable for the building they were quarried for. These stones are then stacked, side by side, and on top of one another in alternating patterns to form a wall. Next, the wall is solidified with cement. This continues on until a structure is completed. This process has a deeper moral and philosophical meaning to Speculative Freemasonry. We all begin our Masonic life as rough ashlars. The rough ashlar is a symbol of our dependence on material things, on our dependence on our passions and desires to rules our actions, and our separation from God in our daily lives. Just as this crude-looking stone is not fit to be used in a structure, this rough stone is not fit as a piece of our character in our inner temple we are spiritually building. We must use the symbols given to us throughout our degrees to shape the makeup of our character into pieces more suitable for our spiritual temple within ourselves. Decoding this symbolism serves as a reminder to us individually as we shape our character, and to us collectively as we build and improve our Lodge.

The Operative Art

From a literal point of view, ashlars begin as raw stone, which are cut, or hewn from a quarry. This produces a slightly oversized, but very rough-looking cubical stone.₆ Care must be given at this point in selecting which area to quarry. Not all stone is created equal. There could be fissures, voids, or some other material weakness in an area

22

of the quarry. Once an area is selected, rock is removed into rough, cubical objects. Now that we have crude ashlars to shape, the Apprentice gets to work. It is his job, based on the working tools given to him, to measure and shape the stone. He uses the 24-inch gauge to measure the ashlar and determine what area should be removed. The Apprentice then takes up the common gavel, and begins chipping away the extra, or unnecessary stone. He constantly switches between these two tools, going between analysis and action4, until at last he feels the cube is ready. The ashlar is then presented to the Fellow Craft who checks after the Apprentice with the working tools of his degree. Every vertical surface is tested with the plumb, to ensure an even and upright surface from top to bottom. He then takes up the level and checks every horizontal surface for the same qualities across from side to side. Finally, with the square, he checks every right angle to ensure an exact 90° angle is maintained throughout the stone. If any adjustment should be made, the ashlar is sent back to the Apprentice to further work the stone until perfection is reached on every facet and every angle of the cube. Lastly, all perfect ashlars are carried to the construction site, where the workers place the stone at the direction of the Master Mason, who uses his working tool, the trowel, to solidify the wall being built by spreading cement throughout all joints between the stone, until at last a collection of perfected cubical stones become a single wall. The Master Mason utilizes the third movable jewel, the trestle board, to place the stones according to the design thereon.6 This continues until the temple walls are completed, and the temple itself is constructed.

For the Individual Mason

A man may step away from the "quarry" of humanity. Separating himself with a desire for something different, something more. This may initially be curiosity. Sometimes, he is seeking a deeper meaning to his life, and thinks Freemasonry may have the answer. He may know something about the Fraternity, but he wants to see what it is all about. He may have even done extensive research online and may have a good foundation in his mind of what our Fraternity can teach him. He has hopefully chosen to step forward and petition a Lodge for the right reasons. He is deemed worthy to receive the degrees of Masonry. Afterwards, he begins his work.

Throughout the degrees, this man is taught lessons and shown tools which serve as reminders of how to shape a moral and upright man. The ashlars he quarries are the internal attributes of his character. These attributes are rough and misshapen at first, which represents that his actions may still be under the influence of the material world and his passions. Think back to the literal description of working an ashlar. The Apprentice chipped away needless stone, then measured his work with the gauge. This makes the distinction that we do not always act; we must sometimes contemplate our past as well as our future actions. By the same token, we cannot stay in a state of constant analysis; we must sooner or later act, and should do so morally. If we are chipping away those actions and thoughts which are not in line with a high character, what is left must be actions and thoughts of rightness. The Apprentice uses the tool of action, the common gavel, as he chips away "all of the vices and superfluities of life,"[1] shaping his actions in accordance with virtues of rightness[4]. He works the traits of his character until he has effectively ridded himself of the actions and thoughts of a material person, one who succumbs to his passions, or one who is not spiritually connected to God. The 24-inch gauge, a tool of analysis[4], is said to help a Mason properly divide his time among service to God and a distressed, worthy brother, his vocations, and refreshment and sleep. Just as the gauge was used to determine the size of the stone worked, it can also be thought of as his initial measure of rightness. The gauge is thus a tool to measure the extent of a man's morality against the makeup of his character.

What can be meant by a man's rightness? The working tools of the Fellow Craft show us what this entails. After passing, a man uses the lessons taught by these new working tools to compare his actions to the ideal. According to the *Louisiana Masonic Monitor,* the plumb, "which, like Jacob's ladder, connects heaven and earth, is the criterion of rectitude and truth. It teaches us to walk justly and uprightly before God and man, turning neither to the right nor to the left from the strict trials of virtue." The level "demonstrates that we are all sprung from the same stock, partake of the same nature, and share the same hope... He who is placed on the lowest spoke of Fortune's wheel is equally entitled to our regard; for a time will come, and the best and wisest of us know not how soon, when all distinctions save those of goodness and virtue shall cease, and Death, the grand leveler of all human greatness, shall reduce us to the same estate." The square "teaches us to regulate our lives and actions according to Masonic line and rule, and so to harmonize our conduct in this life as to render us acceptable to that Divine Being from whom all goodness springs and to whom we must give an account of all our actions."[1] The square, as it is used to measure the angles of an ashlar, is used to measure the exactness of our virtues and morality. There are four cardinal virtues: fortitude, prudence, temperance, and justice. These virtues were first found in Plato's *Republic* Book IV[2], and can be found in the Old Testament. In addition, there are three theological virtues, described in *1 Corinthians 13* as faith, hope, and charity, or love: "And now abideth faith, hope, charity, these three; but the greatest of these is charity."[3] These seven virtues should also sound very familiar to any Freemason. And so, the square becomes the ultimate guide to his thoughts and actions, as these seven traits are what are measured in his character by its edges. The plumb measures his deviation from each of these ideals, while the level measures whether or not he applies these principles to everyone equally and justly. He works every stone of his character with these tools, analyzing, working, and checking each until all are perfected.

He then stacks these "inner stones" to begin erecting walls of his character. The Master Mason has laid out his designs on the trestle board, and by it he has a plan for his Spiritual Temple. He then uses the trowel to spread the cement of brotherly love and affection, which unites the ashlars of his character into a wall, which is repeated until at last, a place worthy of God to dwell is completed within him. As a Master Mason, he has united his inner wall of virtue and morality with the greatest of all virtues, the virtue of love-unconditional, unprejudiced, and unending love for all mankind, especially a brother Mason.

For the Lodge

The symbolism of the working of the ashlar can apply to an entire Lodge as well. This all begins when a man petitions a lodge. As the stone is carefully chosen from the quarry, we must wisely ballot on a man's worthiness to receive the degrees in Masonry. As the stone may contain fissures, voids, or some other weakness, so might a man who petitions Masonry. He may petition for the wrong reasons, such as to attain a perceived position of power or leadership. He may join simply to learn what is so secret about our Fraternity. He may also just not be a good, upstanding person to begin with. This is what makes the Investigative Committee's job so important. They must determine if a man is worthy of the Fraternity, while at the same time answering any questions the man or his family may have about what Freemasonry is, and perhaps more importantly, what it is not. During the layover period, if at all possible, it is good for other brethren to meet a petitioner, so they have a face to the name they are balloting on. Finally, we must all truly ballot for the good of the order to admit good, upstanding men we feel can not only benefit the Fraternity, but the Fraternity can benefit him.

After a man is balloted on and he is initiated, it is time for him to get to work. He has the catechism work he must learn in order to be passed to the degree of Fellow Craft, but he has also just undergone something he has never experienced before. Mentors should not only work with a young brother on his memory work, but help him understand what he has just experienced. They should answer questions as long as they are able, and not only give the new brother some idea of what things in our ritual mean, but also teach him to seek out meanings for himself. That is not to say he should scour the internet or books for answers. An Apprentice or Fellow Craft may spoil what is to come in future degrees. He may also find things that are different in other jurisdictions that would cause confusion for him at first. It is also no secret that there is plenty of garbage information online about Masonry. A young brother may not have the ability to sift through good and bad information. At a minimum, time must be spent in explaining why we do what we do; otherwise, our ritual can become trivialized. It is true that some brothers will have more interest in symbolism and ritual than others, but we must lay some amount of groundwork for each candidate to begin to understand the degrees. Just as our perfect ashlars were all prepared the same and then used for different purposes, so should we be in cultivating younger Masons.

At some point, after the groundwork of a young brother's understanding has been set, we should set him free to pursue his own interests in the Craft₅. There are brothers who enjoy ritual, while there are others who enjoy fellowship, or charity, or involvement in appendant bodies. Some enjoy all of the above. Back to our literal example, every stone was prepared the same, but used for different purposes. Some were for exterior walls, while others were for interior rooms. Some were for hallways or dining halls, while others were for the Sanctum Sanctorum. It is important that a Brother find his place and be given the ability to excel, all while acting by the character shaped for him by our ritual and lessons. As the five orders of

Architecture teach us there are many different ways to build our own spiritual temple and we must not build idly, so must we encourage new brothers to find their path to keep them involved and prevent burnout or disinterest.

Support and encouragement are also a two-way street. Younger Masons should also support and help the older Masons. They have helped hold together the Fraternity that went from the heyday of yesteryear to the struggles of the last few decades quantity-wise, and deserve our appreciation in holding the Fraternity together5. They are a source of information and should help guide the younger brothers in the Craft. Younger Masons who enjoy ritual and are capable of learning it should do so in order to relieve some of the work that is put on older brethren in conferring degrees. Tasks such as cleanup and meal preparation should be handled more by younger men as much as possible so that our older brethren do not have to be on their feet as much. Younger Masons should take on more responsibility with holding office positions and sitting on committees, not only to learn how the Lodge operates, but to further help and assist older brethren. Older brethren, at the same time, should not be afraid of change or different points of view. Men are drawn to Masonry for all different kinds of reasons, and as much as is possible, we should respect and cultivate those interests. There is room in our great Fraternity for all walks of brethren, and we should always practice the great meaning of the trowel and unite these different men into one common mass with brotherly love and affection.

Conclusion

Freemasonry is not always clear or obvious in its meanings. Sometimes, meanings in symbols must be sought by each of us. There is rarely a case in our Fraternity where one symbol means only one thing, and these symbols can have not only a "textbook" meaning, but also different, yet meaningful and unique meanings to each individual.

Another point to remember about these symbols is that we are constantly surrounded by them during Communications and Degrees, and we should contemplate and remember their meaning. Freemasonry is meant to be practiced individually, as a collective group within a Lodge, as a collective group of Lodges at a Grand Lodge, and outside of Masonic gatherings in our everyday life. It is important to note that a perfect ashlar is impossible to accomplish in this life. We are mortal, and as such, we will always fall short of the ideal. It is the journey to this perfect ashlar that matters. We will improve ourselves as we shape our stone. The meanings of the rough and perfect ashlars, and how our working tools can be applied to these ashlars, are not only poignant lessons for our own inner spiritual development, but can help brethren remember how each member of a Lodge should be cultivated and cared for to make the Lodge the best it can be.

(*Special thanks to MWB Lloyd E. Hennigan, Jr, Past Grand Master of Masons 2008, Grand Lodge of Louisiana, Free & Accepted Masons, for his input and review of this paper*)

Bibliography

1. Huckaby, G.C. (compiled by). *The Louisiana Monitor of the Degrees Entered Apprentice, Fellow Craft, and Master Mason and Other Masonic Ceremonies.* 26th Ed. Fine Print, Alexandria, LA/Grand Lodge of the State of Louisiana, F. & A.M., 1988.
2. Plato, *Republic,* Book IV, Loeb Classical Library, Harvard University Press, February 4, 2013.
3. *Holy Bible: King James Version, 1 Corinthians, Chapter 13.* DeVore & Sons, Inc. Wichita, KS. 1988.
4. MacNulty, Kirk W. *The Way of the Craftsman: A Search for the Spiritual Essence of Craft Freemasonry.* Plumbstone Publishing, Washington DC. May 1, 2017.
5. Poll, Michael R. "Our Changing Freemasonry." New Orleans Scottish Rite College. New Orleans, LA. September 21, 2019
6. Roberts, Allen E. *The Craft & Its Symbols: Opening the Door to Masonic Symbolism.* Macoy Publishing & Masonic Supply Company, Inc. Richmond, VA, 1974.

The Elimination of the French Influence in Louisiana Masonry
By Michael R. Poll

Unlike other areas of the United States, Masonry did not begin in Louisiana with the introduction of British styled Masonry. Louisiana was originally established as a French territory. The French culture remained in Louisiana throughout the Spanish reign and also after the area became part of the United States. As a result, the Masons of Louisiana, logically, favored French styled Masonry. However, with the influx of "Americans" and the American culture, British styled Masonry began to grow in significance in the state. These two influences created a unique situation in Louisiana. While Perfect Union Lodge (long believed to be Louisiana's first Masonic lodge[1]) obtained its charter as a York Rite (American-Webb) Lodge from the Grand Lodge of Ancient York Masons of South Carolina in 1793, the Lodge worked in the French language (as did the Grand Lodge from its birth in 1812 until 1850) and was French in nature. Just prior to the formation of the Grand Lodge of Louisiana, the only two English speaking lodges in New Orleans (Louisiana and Harmony) withdrew from the Masonic convention created to form the Grand Lodge. This resulted in the Grand Lodge being formed by five French-speaking Lodges.[2]

As the steady stream of English-speaking "Americans" came into New Orleans the impact was felt on both the New Orleans culture and New Orleans Masonry in general. The English-speaking Masons who came to New Orleans were, by vast majority, of the York Rite (American Preston/Webb Ritual) and found little interest in the French-speaking New Orleans Masonic lodges. The developing conflict between the various Masonic Rites in New Orleans (French, Scottish, and York) can be viewed as a conflict between the co-existing New Orleans cultures. The established French-speaking population did not wish to relinquish its dominance over either the cities' culture or Masonry. The English-speaking citizens of New Orleans (outnumbering the French-speaking citizens by the 1830's) felt that their needs were not being accommodated by the then minority French establishment. Revolt was inevitable.

In January 1833, a concordat was entered into between the Grand Consistory of Louisiana and the Grand Lodge of Louisiana.[3] This event can be seen as the catalyst for the schism in Louisiana Masonry that was soon to take place. In order to attempt to understand the significance of this concordat and the reasons behind it, a brief history of the Grand Consistory of Louisiana is necessary.

The Grand Consistory of Louisiana was organized and chartered in 1811 by the Supreme Council at Kingston, Jamaica.[4] Upon Louisiana achieving statehood in 1812, the Grand Consistory would seem to be no longer in a territory that could be considered "open" and could no longer remain under the jurisdiction of a foreign supreme council. Since fraternal relations between the Supreme Councils at Charleston and Kingston existed,[5] it would be logical to assume that the Grand Consistory would pass under the jurisdiction of the Charleston Council. However, this did not happen. The Grand Consistory (or, at least, part of it) passed under the jurisdiction of the Cerneau Bodies in New York in 1813 (considered irregular by the Charleston Council). At this point, the *Grand Consistory of Louisiana* reorganized into the *Grand Council of Louisiana*.[6] Why would the Grand Consistory make this seemingly unusual move and place itself under a supreme council that was considered irregular? The answer may come from the fact that the Cerneau Council was composed of members of the regular Grand Lodge of New York. DeWitt Clinton was a long time Grand Master of New York, held in very high regard, *and* was the Deputy Grand Commander of the Cerneau Council. The Charleston Council was composed of members of the then irregular Grand Lodge of South Carolina.[7] The only logical answer for the Grand Consistory's action was that it considered *Charleston* to be the irregular supreme council. The Grand Consistory of Louisiana was not the only body to begin favoring the Cerneau bodies over the Charleston Council. The Grand Commander of the Supreme Council of Kingston Jamaica, J.J. Itter, is listed as an Honorary member of the Cerneau Sovereign Grand Consistory in the 1818 register of members.[8] This register is reprinted in Folger's *Ancient and Accepted Scottish Rite in Thirty-three Degrees* and carries the note:

> *This Pamphlet is annexed because it is a much more perfect one, than those published in 1813, 1814, 1815, and 1816. The others are not as full, and this is precisely like the preceding ones in every respect, the Author has preferred the one of this date.*[9]

While it is dangerous to draw the conclusion that Itter was an Honorary Member of the Cerneau Sovereign Grand Consistory from its creation based on Folger's unverified statement, J.J.J. Gourgas wrote to Emanuel De La Motta on 3 July 1815:

> *... we have one [communication] which says that I.I. [sic, read J.J.] Itter, the Sn. Gr. Cr. there, loves money much, is a second Joseph Cerneau there and entirely devoted to him, that it is needful to take precautions for the correspondence with the Supe. Gd. Council, and even that the said Itter is the grand director and manager of everything; it is recommended, however, as a precaution, to correspond and direct to Ill. Br. Morales, formerly the Sn. Gd. Comr., &c., &c., &c ...* [10]

It does seem that the Supreme Council in Jamaica (or, at least, part of it) had switched to the Cerneau camp.

The battles between the Cerneau Council and the Councils in the Southern and Northern Jurisdictions (and additionally the problems resulting from the anti-masonic movements across the U.S.) would soon take its toll on all of the U.S. supreme councils. By the late 1820's the Cerneau Council fell apart and soon died. John Holland, who was long time Grand Master of the Grand Lodge of Louisiana and Commander in Chief of the Grand Council of Louisiana, sought in vain to contact the Cerneau Council. When it became clear that the Cerneau Council was no longer active (and after having received communications from the Council in the Northern Jurisdiction), the Grand Council of Louisiana decided to pass under the jurisdiction of the Charleston Supreme Council in 1831.[11] While under the jurisdiction of the Charleston Council, the renamed Grand *Consistory* of Louisiana chartered two Scottish Rite Symbolic Lodges (*Les Trinosophes & La Liberale*) most likely using Emanuel De La Motta'a 1814 *Rejoinder* as their justification.[12] With the growing friction between the two New Orleans cultures, the French controlled Grand Consistory might, also, have taken this action to carve out a strong hold not only for the French speaking concerns, but, also, the Scottish Rite. It should be noted that while relations between the French and English-speaking Masons of New Orleans were of a volatile nature, the relations between the French speaking French Rite and French speaking Scottish Rite Masons were, also, in a deteriorating state. The Grand Lodge, at that time, was strongly influenced by the French Rite,[13] and clearly did not want to see control of symbolic lodges lost to the Grand Consistory. In 1833, a concordat was entered into between the Grand Consistory and the Grand Lodge whereby the Grand Lodge would issue symbolic charters for the York, French, and Scottish Rite and provide Symbolic Chambers for the management of the various lodges in the Grand Lodge. In exchange, the Grand Consistory relinquished its right to charter symbolic lodges. This might have settled some of the problems existing between the French and Scottish Rites, but it only created more problems between the French and English-speaking Masons.

By the early 1830's the Charleston Council appeared to have met the same fate as the Cerneau Council.[14] On 1 September 1832, the Marquis de St. Angelo visited the Grand Consistory and explained the state of affairs of High Degree Scottish Rite Masonry in the U.S. He announced that the United Supreme Council of the Western Hemisphere had been organized and informed them of the benefits of passing under its jurisdiction.[15] Obviously realizing that this Council was a reorganization of the Cerneau Council and that the Charleston Council in the Southern Jurisdiction and the De La Motta Council in the Northern Jurisdiction were no longer active, the Grand Consistory resolved to pass under St. Angelo's Council on the same day of his visit. Once again, it must be realized that Cerneau Masonry was not universally deemed irregular at this time. Lafayette had been well received by the Grand Lodge of Louisiana on 14 April 1825. Just eight months earlier, on 15 August 1824, the Cerneau Council conferred the 33° on Lafayette and, despite contradictory statements by the Charleston Council,[16] he considered *himself* a Cerneau Mason until his death in May of 1834.[17] Unfortunately, the United Supreme Council of the Western Hemisphere (despite entering into a treaty with the Supreme Council of France in 1834)[18] was not to be a long lived supreme council. In 1839, the Marquis St. Angelo returned to New Orleans as the Lt. Grand Commander of the United Supreme Council of the Western Hemisphere and, due to the near death of that Council, organized the *Supreme Council for the United States of America sitting in New Orleans* on 27 October of that year.[19] The Supreme Council of Louisiana (as it became known) was received by both the Grand Lodge and Grand Consistory of Louisiana and fraternal relations were established between all bodies.[20] The United Supreme Council of the Western Hemisphere lingered on until the early 1840's and then died. On 9 October 1846, the Grand Consistory of Louisiana passed under the Jurisdiction of the Supreme Council of Louisiana.[21]

The English-speaking Masons found no comfort in the Concordat of 1833 nor the fact that a Symbolic Chamber would be created for the management of the three Rites in Louisiana Masonry. The English-speaking Masons felt that the York Rite should be the sole rite in the Grand Lodge. The various activities of the New Orleans Scottish Rite Masons could have been viewed as further evidence of instability in the "French" Masonry. The unrest reached the boiling point in 1844 with the new Constitution for the Grand Lodge of Louisiana. The three Rites were officially recognized by the Constitution and this seemed to be the breaking point for the York Rite Masons. 1844 would, also, be a turning point in Louisiana Masonry for both the Grand Lodge *and* the Scottish Rite bodies.

Ray Baker Harris states: *"Oddly enough, as a revival of the Southern Supreme Council began in Charleston in 1844, in the same year, and completely unrelated and independently, Gourgas and Yates were resuming discussion of the possible revival in the Northern Jurisdiction."*[22] The revived Charleston Council was, undoubtedly, aware of the New Orleans Council as the Council's "birth announcement" survives in the Holbrook papers in the Archives of the Southern Jurisdiction.[23] The Charleston Council neither protested nor took action against the New Orleans Council — at that time. In 1845, a powerful Past Grand Master of the Grand Lodge of Louisiana became the Grand Commander of the Supreme Council of Louisiana. New Orleans Criminal Court Judge Jean Francois Canonge served the Grand Lodge of Louisiana as Grand Master in 1822-24 and 1829 and, also, served as Commander in Chief of the Grand Consistory of Louisiana from 1843-46. Canonge had served as the Grand Senior Warden of the Cerneau Grand Council of Princes of the Royal Secret, 32° in Philadelphia in 1818[24] and was a founding member of the Supreme Council of Louisiana in 1839. It was during his administration that the Grand Consistory passed under the jurisdiction of the Supreme Council of Louisiana. With the influential Canonge as Grand Commander and numerous

Past Grand Masters and Grand Lodge Officers serving as members and officers of both the Grand Consistory and Supreme Council of Louisiana, it is likely that the newly revived and very unstable Charleston Council did not wish (remembering the battles with the New York Cerneau Council) to directly confront the New Orleans Scottish Rite Bodies.

The New Orleans English-speaking York Rite Masons felt that the 1844 Constitution of the Grand Lodge of Louisiana altered the Grand Lodge into a body that was no longer an Ancient York Rite Grand Lodge. The decision was made to sever their association with the Grand Lodge and organize themselves into what they felt was proper York Rite Masonry. A committee was formed, and a letter of grievance was brought before the Grand Lodge of Mississippi on January 23, 1845.[25] The Grand Master of the Grand Lodge of Mississippi was Mexican War hero and former governor of Mississippi, John A. Quitman. The Grand Lodge of Mississippi appointed a committee to go to New Orleans in order to examine the situation. One year later, on January 21, 1846, the committee presented two reports before the Grand Lodge of Mississippi concerning the events in New Orleans. The first report was presented on behalf of the "majority" of the committee:

> *The committee to whom was referred the controversy between the Ancient York Masons of the State of Louisiana, on one side, and the Scotch and French Masons of said State, on the other, have duly considered the subject, and beg leave to report the following resolutions:*
>
> *1. Resolved, That no Grand Lodge of Scotch and French, or Modern Masonry can assume jurisdiction over any Ancient York Mason, or body of such.*
>
> *2. Resolved, That it is not consistent with Ancient York Masonry, to unite with Scotch and Modern Masonry, or either of them, in the formation of a Lodge, Grand or Subordinate.*

3. Resolved, That there is no Grand Lodge of Ancient York Masons within the limits of the State of Louisiana.

4. Resolved, That this Grand Lodge has the power, and it is its duty on proper application, to issue Dispensations and Charters to bodies of Ancient York Masons within the limits of the State of Louisiana, until the constitution of a Grand Lodge within that State.

5. Resolved, That we entertain the highest opinion of the distinguished body known as the Grand Lodge of Louisiana, and are willing to contribute as much as possible, consistent with our obligations, to aid and protect Ancient York Masons, wheresoever dispersed, and to maintain our Order pure and unmingled, to preserve friendly relations with that honorable body.

6. Resolved, That under no possible circumstances would this Grand Lodge assume jurisdiction over a Scotch or Modern Mason, or body of such, such assumption being alike inconsistent with their rights and our principles.

DUDLEY S. JENNINGS, R. N. DOWNING, J. J. DOTY, Committee [26]

The undersigned, a member of the committee to whom was referred so much of the Address of the M. W Grand Master, as relates to the M. W Grand Lodge of Louisiana, and also the verbal report of the committee appointed to visit that M. W. Body, begs leave to state by way of minority report, That the M. W. Grand Lodge of the State of Louisiana was organized exclusively after the Ancient York Rite, and so remained for a number of years, until it accumulated the Scotch and French Rites. Said Grand Lodge is constituted by free and voluntary meetings of the Subordinate Lodges of the State, represented for life by the Master of each Lodge, who has presided over his Lodge for one year, and temporally by the Senior and Junior Wardens. According to the information now before the undersigned, there are now in active operation fourteen Lodges working in the Ancient York Rite; four in the Scotch Rite, accumulating the York and Modern Rite, and two in the Modern Rite, accumulating the Scotch and York Rite.

The undersigned would further respectfully submit, that no one of the fourteen Lodges above named, (as the undersigned believes,) has made any official complaint to this body of any improper or unmasonic conduct on the part of the M. W. Grand Lodge of Louisiana.

The undersigned is aware of the fact that St. Albans Lodge, No. 28, Louisiana, did, on the 9th July last issue a circular, addressed to the York Lodges in that State, requesting them to meet in convention and form a Grand Lodge of York Masons. The undersigned has yet to learn that more than one other Lodge of the State of Louisiana accepted or acted on the proposition of the said St. Albans Lodge. The undersigned would further represent that the M. W. Grand Lodge of Louisiana was constituted exclusively in the York Rite, that it is still a York Rite Grand Lodge, accumulating the Scotch and Modern Rite; that it grants charters authorizing Masonic work and labor in the York Rite exclusively, and that it also grants charters authorizing work in either the Scotch or French Rite, but invariably requires, in the later cases, that the York Rite shall always be communicated upon the candidate for the degrees in the latter Lodges. All the Masons of Louisiana are thus strictly Ancient York, though many of them possess also the French and Scotch Rite. These Rites obtain generally throughout the world, and any reflection upon the organization of the M. W. Grand Lodge of Louisiana would equally reflect upon the conduct and proceedings of the Supreme Bodies of Masonry in France, Scotland and other nations, where these Rites are peculiarly esteemed. The undersigned would respectfully submit that this Grand Lodge do respectfully and fraternally remonstrate with the M.W. Grand Lodge of Louisiana *upon its tolerance or the use by its Subordinate Lodges of ***** or their peculiar charts. The following resolutions are submitted:*

1. Resolved, That this Grand Lodge finds nothing in the proceedings of the M. W. Grand Lodge of Louisiana, which demands a termination of the Masonic relations heretofore existing between them.

2. Resolved, That this Grand Lodge would not, (at least under present circumstances,) feel itself justified in granting Dispensations or Charters to any body of Masons in the State of Louisiana.

All of which is respectfully submitted,

H.W. Walter [27]

A second "counter" report was made, but the outcome of the events of 21 January (despite the efforts of the two "counter" reports) was the chartering of George Washington Lodge in New Orleans and Lafayette Lodge in Lafayette[28] by the Grand Lodge of Mississippi on 22 February. Relations were severed between the Grand Lodges of Louisiana and Mississippi and the Louisiana Lodges chartered by the Grand Lodge of Mississippi were declared clandestine by the Grand Lodge of Louisiana. In total, the Grand Lodge of Mississippi would charter seven Lodges in New Orleans by 1848.[29] These seven Lodges would unite to form the *Louisiana Grand Lodge of Ancient York* Masons on March 8th, 1848. The Grand Lodge of Mississippi received admonishes from most U.S. Grand Lodges and the majority openly condemned its action.[30] While the future for this splinter group of the Grand Lodge of Louisiana may have looked bleak, several events would take place to not only strengthen the position of the English-speaking New Orleans Masons but assure them of total victory and the loss of French control over *all* forms of Louisiana Masonry.

19 January 1848 would bring the death of Jean-Francois Canonge, the Grand Commander of the Supreme Council of Louisiana. In his place would be elected James Foulhouze as Grand Commander. Foulhouze had been appointed Grand

Secretary of the Supreme Council in 1847[31] and had received his 33° only two years earlier from the Supreme Council of the Grand Orient of France.[32] The election of Foulhouze as Grand Commander bypassed a number of senior members of the Council and, clearly, established the popularity of Foulhouze with the Council. Foulhouze had brought with him various rituals from France[33] which he rewrote for the New Orleans Council.[34] Foulhouze was a brilliant man who would soon be elected as a District Court Judge. The former Roman Catholic priest turned lawyer and Mason was obviously recognized as possessing great ability with Masonic philosophy and high organization and leadership ability (as his later battles with the Charleston Council would prove). Foulhouze was not, however, a Past Grand Master and his influence in the Grand Lodge was limited. During the same month as the death of Canonge, the Charleston Council was talking an action that would greatly strengthen its own position and further weaken the hold of the French-speaking New Orleans Masons. Albert Mackey (the Grand Secretary of the Charleston Council) sent a notice to the *Freemason's Monthly Magazine*[35] (Boston) which read:

> *At a special session of the Supreme Council ... for the Southern Jurisdiction of the United States of America, our Illustrious Brother John A. Quitman ... Major General in the Army of the United States, was elected to fill a vacancy in this Supreme Council, and was duly and formally inaugurated a Sovereign Grand Inspector General of the 33d. All Consistories, Councils, Chapters and Lodges under this jurisdiction are hereby ordered to obey and respect him accordingly.*[36]

It is interesting to note that at the same special session of the Charleston Council (or very soon after) Achille Le Prince was elected as a S.G.I.G.[37] yet no notice in a national masonic magazine was apparently published. It is, also, interesting to examine the selection of Quitman as a member of the Charleston Council. Obviously, Quitman was a powerful and well-known individual who would be an asset to the Charleston Council, but would his actions against the Grand Lodge of Louisiana be a source of embarrassment to the Charleston Council? In December of 1848 the Grand Lodge of South Carolina issued a statement and a resolution concerning the actions of the Grand Lodge of Mississippi. The South Carolina Committee considered all points of the arguments of the Grand Lodges of Louisiana and Mississippi. While it did not condone the cumulating of rites by the Grand Lodge of Louisiana and hoped that *"the anomaly of mixed rites will be abolished by the Grand Lodge of Louisiana,"*[38] it also found no cause for the Grand Lodge of Mississippi to *"invade"* the jurisdiction of the Grand Lodge of Louisiana. In addition, the report states:

> Your committee sincerely regret that by the formation of another Grand Lodge in the City of New Orleans, there has been another flagrant violation of the rights of the Grand Lodge of Louisiana. This new body is under the title of Louisiana Grand Lodge of Ancient York Masons. [39]
>
> Resolved that the Grand Lodge of Louisiana did not forfeit their right of jurisdiction in Louisiana by the course they adopted in cumulating the degrees, altho this Grand Lodge disapproves of such improper acts and mal practices, and is desirous to learn that they have been abolished; and the ancient landmarks restored.
>
> Resolved that the Grand Lodge of Mississippi, in granting warrants to establish new Grand Lodges within the State of Louisiana, made a premature and unlawful entry into a foreign jurisdiction which was not warranted by the occasion, and, to say the least, was a violation of that courtesy, which ought to exist between Grand Lodges.
>
> Resolved that without speedy conclusion to the differences between two Grand Lodges now erected in Louisiana, the Grand Lodges throughout the United States ought to adopt some stringent method of

depriving one, or the other, of the right of assuming
authority which certainly only one is entitled to.
    A E. Miller, J.H. Honour,
    Z.B. Oakes, J.G. Norris, J.C. Barber.* [40]

While the resolution of the Grand Lodge of South
Carolina was not harshly critical of the Grand Lodge of
Mississippi and did place some of the blame on Louisiana, it
is *most* significant that *any* criticism, at all, of Mississippi by
the Grand Lodge of South Carolina occurred. Two of the five
members of the Grand Lodge of South Carolina committee
were also Active Members of the Charleston Supreme
Council. J.C. Norris was the Grand Treasurer and J.H.
Honour was Grand Commander! When the officers of the
Charleston Supreme Council and the officers of the Grand
Lodge of South Carolina for 1848 are compared an
interesting picture is painted.

John H. Honour—Grand Commander of Charleston
Council & Grand Treasurer of Grand Lodge; Charles M.
Furman—Lt. Grand Commander of Charleston Council &
Grand Master of Grand Lodge (1838-40,1847-48); James
Norris—Grand Treasurer of Charleston Council & Past
Grand Master of Grand Lodge (1846); Albert G. Mackey—
Grand Secretary of Charleston Council & Grand Secretary of
Grand Lodge ; James Burges—S. G. I. G. in Charleston
Council & Grand Senior Warden of Grand Lodge; Achille Le
Prince—S. G. I. G. in Charleston Council & no elected office
in Grand Lodge; William S. Rockwell—S.G.I.G. from
Georgia; John R. McDaniel—S.G.I.G. from Virginia; John A.
Quitman—S.G.I.G. from Mississippi

Out of the 6 member of the Charleston Council that
lived in South Carolina only *one* was not a high-ranking
Grand Lodge Officer. The *Grand Master*, Charles M. Furman,
was the Lt. Grand Commander of the Charleston Council.
Stating that the Grand Lodge of Mississippi had acted
improperly was admitting that a newly elected Sovereign
Grand Inspector General of the Charleston Council had
acted improperly *prior* to his election. Why then was

Quitman elected to this office? In fairness to the Charleston Council, it must be noted that a man should not be condemned before all of the evidence is examined. Quitman was made an Active Member of the Charleston Council nearly a year before the Grand Lodge made its rulings on Quitman's Grand Lodge. It must also be noted that the Charleston Council was not obligated to act in harmony with the Grand Lodge of South Carolina nor have the same agenda. The Grand Lodge of South Carolina was, in no way, threatened by the existence of *any* Masonic body in New Orleans. The Charleston Council, however, was *very much* threatened by the well-organized "Cerneau" New Orleans Scottish Rite bodies — the *only* Scottish Rite Bodies in the U.S. to remain active during the "dormant" period of the Supreme Councils of the Northern and Southern jurisdictions.[41] While wearing the "Supreme Council" hat, Grand Commander John Honour, as well as the other Charleston Council members, were obligated to do all in their power to assure that the Charleston Council would survive. This included recruiting the powerful and very influential John Quitman. While wearing the "Grand Lodge" hat, John Honour and the rest of the Grand Lodge were obligated to chastise Quitman (although not mentioning his name) through the unwarranted actions of the Grand Lodge of Mississippi (actions which, however, would ultimately prove helpful to the Charleston Council).

The Louisiana Grand Lodge of Ancient York Masons was organized on March 8, 1848 and was recognized by only one other Grand Lodge — The Grand Lodge of Mississippi. In 1849, John Gedge was elected Grand Master of the Louisiana Grand Lodge of Ancient York Masons. Despite the regularity question of the Louisiana Grand Lodge and the lack of support for this new Grand Lodge around the world, the Grand Lodge of Louisiana merged with this body in 1850. The Grand Lodge of Louisiana was left with little choice in this matter. The fact that the Grand Lodge of Louisiana was overwhelmingly considered the "regular" Grand Lodge was not sufficient to overcome the internal problems stemming from the cultural divisions in New Orleans. By mid-1849, it was realized that the English-speaking lodges that had remained loyal to the Grand Lodge were showing signs that continued loyalty would, most likely, not happen. The division between the French-speaking Scottish and French Rite New Orleans Masons only contributed to the dilemma. Obviously realizing that the total collapse of the Grand Lodge of Louisiana was a very real possibility, the Grand Lodge of Louisiana and the Louisiana Grand Lodge entered into talks designed to merge the two bodies.[42] That merger took place in June of 1850 with the approval of a new Constitution of the *Grand Lodge of Louisiana of Free and Accepted Masons*. Under the terms of the agreement of the merger, the Louisiana Grand Lodge members declared irregular would be declared "regular" by the Grand Lodge of Louisiana. All Lodges chartered by the Louisiana Grand Lodge (or by the Grand Lodge of Mississippi in Louisiana) would, also, pass under the jurisdiction of the new Grand Lodge of Louisiana. The one phrase that was agreed upon that would result in *great* unrest with the French-speaking New Orleans Masons was Article II Section 2 which read: *It* [the Grand Lodge of Louisiana] *is constituted as a Grand Lodge of Free and Accepted Masons, and in that capacity recognizes nothing but pure Ancient Free Masonry, consisting of the three symbolic degrees of Apprentice, Fellow Craft and Master Mason, and is forbidden to tolerate any distinctions derogatory to the character in which it is constituted.*[43] Believing that this phrase would result in the Grand Lodge of Louisiana maintaining its former position concerning the several rites in New Orleans, the French speaking New Orleans Masons agreed to the new Constitutions. After the Constitution was passed, the "new" Grand Lodge of Louisiana (then controlled by the English-speaking Masons announced that "pure Ancient Free Masonry" was the equivalent of "Ancient York Rite Masonry." All non-York Rite Lodges were instructed to turn in their charters in order to receive new York Rite charters.[44] The French-speaking New Orleans Masons flew into rage.

Charges of trickery abounded. Two French-speaking Lodges (Polar Star and Disciples of the Masonic Senate) and a Spanish-speaking Lodge (Los Amigos del Order) applied to the Supreme Council of Louisiana for relief. The Supreme Council of Louisiana announced that since the Concordat of 1833 between the Grand Lodge of Louisiana and the Grand Consistory of Louisiana (at that time the highest ranking body of Scottish Rite Masons in the State) had been violated by the Grand Lodge, the Supreme Council would have no choice but to issue Scottish Rite charters to the subordinate Scottish Rite Symbolic Lodges.[45]

If the goal of the new 1850 Grand Lodge Constitution and the merger with the Louisiana Grand Lodge was to bring peace to *all* the Louisiana Masons, it was a total failure. If the goal was to remove the power base in the Grand Lodge from the French-speaking New Orleans Masons, it was, indeed, a success. The French-speaking New Orleans Masons became split after 1850. One faction, outraged at the turn of events, wished nothing more to do with the Grand Lodge and saw the Supreme Council as the only hope of maintaining the French interests. The other French faction, most likely simply tired of the squabbles, remained with the Grand Lodge in the hopes of possibly still bringing unity to the troubled Grand Lodge. In 1851, John Gedge, who two years earlier was the Grand Master of the irregular Louisiana Grand Lodge, was elected Grand Master of the Grand Lodge of Louisiana. Any thought that the "new" Grand Lodge of Louisiana was *not* under the control of the English-speaking Masons was clearly eliminated. The Grand Lodge and Supreme Council, once closely related bodies, were now opposing forces. With Louisiana Masonry in a state of turmoil and the once powerful Supreme Council of Louisiana fighting for order and realizing that it was no longer a stable authority, the time for the Charleston Council to act was at hand.

At the invitation of John Gedge, Albert Mackey came to New Orleans in 1852 and established, for the Charleston Supreme Council, a Consistory of the 32°. Obviously, the

New Orleans Scottish Rite bodies charged that this was an outrageous invasion of territory. Not only was the fact that the Consistory was organized in New Orleans, but the manner in which it was created was the subject of severe criticism. James Foulhouze would comment in his *Historical Inquiry:*

> *Gedge knew where the deception lay, and that it was no accident but the result of artful design. He hated the Scotch Rite, and had attempted all in his power to destroy it. The question therefore for him was to find out how he could carry out his purpose, and he was unscrupulous about the means to employ, he conceived the idea of becoming a Scotch Mason himself if it was possible. He succeeded in finding at Charleston a man as unscrupulous as himself, a man of whom one who is now a chief supporter of the Charleston Consistory in Louisiana said in 1853 that an eternal shame should weigh upon him for what he (Mackey) then did. That man was A.G. Mackey. He came at Gedge's request to establish a Consistory for the government of the supreme power at Charleston, appointing Gedge as the Commander, and therein conferring the High Degrees of what they are pleased to call the Scotch Rite in a manner as to create disgust even to those who now exalt him as their most potent monarch, if we may believe the same authority.* [46]

James Foulhouze is usually judged unkindly by most Masonic historians (either fairly or unfairly). Foulhouze, clearly had little use for the Charleston Supreme Council and his anger at the Charleston Council is evident. These facts aside, this statement by Foulhouze should be examined for accuracy. Foulhouze claimed that an unnamed Charleston supporter charged that the manner in which the "Mackey" Consistory was created was an "eternal shame" on those conferring the degrees. That unnamed Mason was Charles Laffon de Ladebat, 33°. After the Concordat of 1855 merging the New Orleans and Charleston Councils, Ladebat would become an Active Member and Officer in the Charleston Council. In 1853, Ladebat wrote about the Grand Lodge events of 1850 and the new Consistory as follows:

> *In presence of such despotic, anti-masonic conduct, the Scotch BB.: resisted as men, as Masons, and formed an independent corporation under the only M.: authority existing in Louisiana "de jure et de facto." The balance remained with the new Grand Lodge, swore obedience to her, through indifference rather than from conviction. Soon after this, the very same Sectarian [John Gedge], in his restlessness, caused Br.: Albert G. Mackey to come from Charleston, in order to establish a Grand Consistory, exactly as if there never had existed a Supreme Council of the Scotch Rite in Louisiana. Our sectarian, after abolishing the Scotch Rite, wished to re-establish it in order to be at the head of it. This Consistory has been inaugurated, you know it M.: W:, for you were admitted into it for proper causes. The manner in which the degrees were conferred in this spurious Consistory is and will be an eternal shame to the Br.: who has conferred them.*[47]

The same anger and emotion that is contained in the Foulhouze quotation is, also, present in this statement by Ladebat. It was, clearly, a time of high emotion and divided passions. From these two quotations, it is not only apparent that the New Orleans Scottish Rite Masons disapproved of the creation of a Charleston Consistory in New Orleans, but they found something very disturbing in the *manner* in which the Scottish Rite degrees were conferred on the members of this New Orleans/Charleston Consistory. To understand Ladebat's "eternal shame" statement we must attempt to trace the possible source of the problem. The following circumstances should be noted:

The Charleston Council, at the time of its creation, worked a different form of the present 33-degree system. The *1802 Charleston Manifesto lists* the 29° as *Knight Kadosh* and the 30°, 31°, and 32° all as *Prince of the Royal Secret.*[48]

The New Orleans Council (as did the Grand Consistory of Louisiana) worked a complete 33 degree system with the degrees as they exist today (29° — *Knight of St. Andrew,* 30° — *Knight Kadosh; 31°* — *Grand Inspector Inquisitor Commander,* 32° — *Prince of the Royal Secret).*[49]

In the 1845 *Charleston Manifesto,* the Charleston Council lists the names of the Council's degrees nearly as they appeared in the *1802 Manifesto.* The 1845 *Manifesto* suggests that the revived Charleston Council had possibly not revised its rituals or did not have possession of its revised rituals.[50]

The Charter for the 1852 "Mackey" Consistory in New Orleans lists the bulk of the degrees exactly as listed in the 1845 & 1802 Manifestos including the 29° as the K-H degree. The 30°, however, is listed as Knight of St. Andrew, 31° — Grand Inquiring Commander and the 32° — Sublime Prince of the Royal Secret.[51]

On March 20, 1853, Albert Mackey *communicated* the degrees from the 4th to the 32nd to Albert Pike at Charleston.[52]

Since Albert Mackey, alone, came to New Orleans and conferred the Scottish Rite degrees from the 4th to the 32nd on the Masons who formed the 1852 New Orleans/Charleston Consistory, it is reasonable to assume that Mackey (like he did with Pike) *communicated* and did not *confer* the degrees. If, in addition to this and the general dissatisfaction of creating a Consistory in an area viewed as "occupied," Mackey used the degree names as listed on the 1852 "Mackey" Consistory, or drastic variations of the known rituals, this could have been viewed by the New Orleans Scottish Rite Masons as an *incredible* deviation from the accepted Scottish Rite manner of initiation and rituals known in New Orleans. The combination of these events could have prompted Ladebat's *"eternal shame"* statement. It is quite clear that the 1852 Consistory flamed the fires and resulted in a "quick burn" of tempers in the French-speaking New Orleans Masons.

The speed and total loss of the Grand Lodge of Louisiana by the French-speaking Masons caused obvious confusion and uncertainty as to the future. Without a powerful leading force, they began to split into factions. James Foulhouze, as Grand Commander, sought to unite all of the French-speaking Masons under his banner. Whether it was because of the rapid advancement of Foulhouze (resulting in uncertainty in his ability) or simply personality conflicts, Foulhouze was not able to unite all of the French Masons. The conflict of opinions within the Supreme Council of Louisiana as to the direction to proceed can reasonably be seen as a contributing factor to the resignation of Foulhouze[53] and nearly all of the officers of the Supreme Council of Louisiana by December of 1853.[54] On 7 January 1854, Charles Claiborne was elected Grand Commander of the Supreme Council of Louisiana. Claude Pierre Samory was elected Lt. Grand Commander and Charles Laffon de Ladebat was appointed Grand Secretary. Samory and Ladebat were part of the French-speaking faction that split from Foulhouze during the 1850-53 turmoil. 1854 was devoted to negotiations with the Charleston Supreme Council. 16 February 1855 the concordat merging the New Orleans and Charleston Supreme Councils was signed in New Orleans. John Gedge, who had spearheaded the movement of the Louisiana Grand Lodge and the 1852 Consistory, would not live to see the concordat between the New Orleans and Charleston Councils — he would die on 13 April 1854.

Claude Pierre Samory would be the first former member of the New Orleans Council to be elected an Active member of the Charleston Council.[55] Following Samory would be Ladebat in 1859.[56] The Grand Consistory of Louisiana would absorb the 1852 Consistory during the Concordat of 1855 and on 17 December 1856, Albert Pike would be unanimously elected commander in chief of the

Grand Consistory of Louisiana — an office that he would hold until his 1859 election as Grand Commander of the Charleston Council.

Ultimately, the French Rite would seemingly disappear from Louisiana Masonry.[57] The French domination of the Grand Lodge and the Scottish Rite Bodies would end.[58] Samory and Ladebat would both move to France in the mid 1860's.[59] The elimination of the French control of Louisiana Masonry was complete. In citing his reasons for his upcoming resignation from the Charleston Council, Charles Laffon de Ladebat summed up the Louisiana situation to Albert Pike in an 1860 letter:

> *My resolution of retiring from active practice is 5 years old & more. Hear what I wrote to Mackey January 31, " When the work will be accomplished, when everything will be in proper order & well understood, I will retire willingly & leave the management of all to more competent but not to more devoted hands." We know that the foreign influence will & must be superseded by the American element. Now that time has come & as I believe that, even in Masonry, Americans must rule in America. I, a frenchman, must retire — in due time.*
>
> *I believe readily that you did not want the office, but the office wanted you & it will be a great pleasure for me to remember ... that I was not the last to devise the means of placing you at the head of the order, 1st by making you a 33rd against the will of Messrs. Furman & Honour: 2nd by vacating my office of Deputy in your favor, & twice you got in the S. C. & especially twice you were unanimously elected to the Presidency, I consider myself as having done my duty, all my duty, all could do. The lifeless council of Charleston was revived; it lives now! Only now tho!* [60]

Notes:

1. The first known Lodge in Louisiana was the Ecossais Lodge *Perfect Harmony* chartered on 16 July 1752 in New Orleans by Perfect Union Lodge in Martinique. *Sharp Document #40* located in the Archives of the Supreme Council Northern Masonic Jurisdiction USA in Lexington Massachusetts. See also: *The Sharp Documents, Volume IV* (Rennes, France: The Latomia Foundation, 1993) 1

2. Perfect Union, Charity, Concorde, Perseverance & Polar Star. All except Charity and Concorde are still active.

3. *Proceedings of the Grand Lodge of the State of Louisiana* (New Orleans: 1848) 16.

4. R.F. Gould, W.J. Hughan, A.F.A. Woodword, D.M. Lyon, J.H. Drummond, E.T. Carson, T.S. Parvin - Editors, *A Library of Freemasonry*, Vol. V (Philadelphia: The John C. Yorston Publishing Co., 1923) 299.

5. Ibid., 298-299.

6. *Minutes Book of the Grand Consistory of Louisiana* (1822-1846). Located in the New Orleans Scottish Rite Bodies. New Orleans, Louisiana. In the Cerneau Scottish Rite, a body of the 32nd degree was called a "Grand Council" and not a "Grand Consistory" as in the Charleston Scottish Rite system.

7. Alain Bernheim, Introduction, *Outline to the Rise and Progress of Freemasonry in Louisiana,* by James B. Scot (New Orleans, LA: Cornerstone Book Publishers, 2008 reprint of 1873 edition) XIV.

8. Robert B. Folger, *The Ancient and Accepted Scottish Rite in Thirty-three Degrees* (New Orleans, Cornerstone Book Publishers, 2011 reprint of 1862 edition) 186.

9. Ibid., 181.

10. *Transactions of the Supreme Council of the 33d Degree for the Southern Jurisdiction USA* (SC SJUSA: Washington, D.C. reprint 1878) 14-16; Alain Bernheim, *Further Light on the Masonic World of Joseph Glock* (London: *Ars Quatuor Coronatorum* Vol. 100, 1987) 46.

11. *Minutes/Grand* Consistory, 21 February 1831 & Bernheim, Introduction, *Outline,* XVI.

12. De La Motta stated: *"I have nothing further to say, except, that although Sublime Masons have not in this country initiated into the Blue or Symbolic Degrees, yet their Councils possess the indefeasible right of granting warrants for that purpose. It is common on the continent of Europe, and may be the case here, should circumstances render the*

exercise of this power necessary. [...] *E. De La Motta, Esq."* Joseph McCosh, *Documents Upon Sublime Freemasonry* (New Orleans, LA: Cornerstone Book Publishers, 2018 reprint of 1823 edition) 62. De La Motta took this statement from Frederick Dalcho's (the Charleston Council's then Lt. Grand Commander) 1803 *Oration*. Bernheim, Introduction, *Outline,* XXIII.

13. Scot, *Outline,* 30, 35.

14. The exact date that the Charleston Council fell dormant cannot be determined.

15. *Minutes Grand Consistory* & Bernheim, Introduction, *Outline, XXV-XXVII.*

16. Harris/Carter, *History,* 158.

17. On 10 May 1834 (ten days before his death), Lafayette wrote in the Golden Book of the United Supreme Council of the Western Hemisphere (held by Comte de St. Laurent) : *I owe today the great favors which the Grand Council of the Western Hemisphere has designed to bestow upon me. I accept them with deep gratitude and will try to merit them through* my zeal. The Lafayette document is in the Archives of the Supreme Council of France. Photocopy in possession of this author. Reprints of this statement are in Julius F. Sachse's *The History of Brother General Lafayette's Fraternal Connections with the R. W. Grand Lodge, F.& A.M., of Pennsylvania* (Philadelphia: The Committee on Library by Resolution of the R.W. Grand Lodge, F.& A.M., of Pennsylvania, 1916) 21 ·23 and Robert Folger's 1862 *Ancient & Accepted Scottish Rite in Thirty-three Degrees* (p. 220). Many thanks to Claude Gagne, 33°, Grand Archivist or the Supreme Council or France, for his assistance.

18. Harris/Carter, *History,* 216.

19. "Birth Announcement" of the Supreme Council of the United States of America Sitting in New Orleans, located in the Archives of the Supreme Council Southern Jurisdiction, USA in Washington, D.C. Photocopy in possession of this author. Scot, *Outline,* 53, 54

20. Ibid 54

21. *Minutes Grand Consistory*, 9 October 1846 & Bernheim, Introduction, *Outline, 29.*

22. Ray Baker Harris, James D. Carter *History of the Supreme Council, 33° Southern Jurisdiction, USA (1801-1861)* Washington, D.C.: The Supreme Council, 33°1964) 224.

23. Ibid., 220.

24. Folger, *Ancient and Accepted Scottish Rite,* 286.

25. *Proceedings of the Grand Lodge of Mississippi A.F.&A.M. 1818-1852* (Jackson, Miss: Clarion Steam Printing Establishment, 1882) 309.

26. Ibid., 320-321.

27. Ibid., 321-322.

28. The town of Lafayette was a suburb of New Orleans in the 1800's located in what is now considered the "uptown" area of New Orleans.

29. George Washington, Lafayette, Warren, Marion, Crescent City, Hiram & Eureka.

30. *Grand Lodge of the State of Louisiana Report and Exposition* (New Orleans: J.L Sollee, 1849) 5-34.

31. James Foulhouze, *Historica/Inquiry* (New Orleans: Cornerstone Book Publishers, 2011 reprint of 1859 edition) 62.

32. Ibid., 60.

33. Charles Laffon de Ladebat, *Ancient and Accepted Rite. Thirtieth Degree* (New Orleans: 1857) xxvii.

34. Charles Laffon-Ladebat states in a footnote of his published 18° ritual: *The philosophical explanation of this and of all the other Degrees from the First up to the Thirtieth inclusive, is taken from the work of Ill.: Bro.: J. Foulhouze, 33d, with some slight alterations, of which, the author willingly assumes the responsibility.* Ladebat, *Ancient and Accepted Scotch Rite. Eighteenth Degree* (New Orleans: 1856) 123. Foulhouze had, also, rewritten the 33° for the Supreme Council of Louisiana. See: James D. Carter, *History of the Supreme Council, 33° SJUSA* (1861-1891) (Washington, D.C.: The Supreme Council 33°, 1967) 37.

35. The title of this magazine is sometimes given as *Freemasons' Magazine.* Many thanks to Alain Bernheim for this discovery.

36. Charles S. Lobingier, *The Supreme Council, 33⁰* (Louisville, KY: The Standard Printing Co., Inc., 1931) 172; Harris/Carter, *History, 236.*

37. Ibid., 236-237.

38. It was the apparent early policy of the Grand Lodge of Louisiana to take a position of non-involvement in areas concerning the rituals of the Lodges under its jurisdiction. In 1844, Germania Lodge #46 was issued a charter as a York Rite German speaking Lodge. Its original German ritual, however, was a mixture of the York, French and Scottish Rites. Arturo de Hoyos, Introduction, *The Liturgy of Germania Lodge No. 46 F.&. A.M.* Translated & edited by Arturo de Hoyos (New Orleans: Michael R. Poll, 1993) v.

39. *Grand Lodge of Louisiana Grand Annual Communication. First Quarterly Session* (New Orleans: J.L. Sollee, 1849) 28-29.

40. Ibid., 28-29.

41. The Cerneau Bodies in New York, the Charleston Supreme Council (SJ) and the De La Motta Supreme Council (NMJ) in New York all ceased being active bodies from a period roughly between the 1820's to mid-1840's. The Grand Consistory of Louisiana remained active during this period of time.

42. Scot, *Outline*, 78-80.

43. *Constitution of the Grand Lodge of the State of Louisiana of Free and Accepted Masons* (New Orleans: The Crescent Office, 1850) 3.

44. Charles Laffon de Ladebat, *The Schism between the Scotch & York Rites* (New Orleans: Cornerstone Book Publishers, 2008 reprint of 1853 edition) 7-8.

45. Scot, *Outline*, 86-87.

46. Foulhouze, *Inquiry*, 62-63.

47. Ladebat, *Letter to Hill*, 9.

48. Harris/Carter, *History*, 319-325.,

49. *1846 General Regulation of the Supreme Council of the USA Sitting in New Orleans. Minutes/Grand* Consistory.

50. Harris/Carter, *History*, 229-231. Note: The Scottish Rite Rituals as transcribed by Albert Pike in 1854 & 55 show the degree structure closer to today's structure, with, for example, the 30° being the K-H degree rather than the 29°. It is possible that Albert Mackey, realizing the problems with the degree structure and reasonably embarrassed by the legitimate uproar of the New Orleans Scottish Rite Masons, restructured the degrees or located them at some point between 1852 and 1854. Thanks to Arturo de Hoyos for information concerning the Pike Manuscript Rituals.

51. A photographic reproduction of the 1852 "Mackey" Consistory is located in the George Longe Paper, Amistad Research Center, Tulane University, New Orleans, LA. A framed copy of this document is also located in the New Orleans Scottish Rite Bodies. New Orleans, Louisiana.

52. Ibid., 244.

53. In his 1858 work, Joseph Lamarre states: *In 1853, Ill. Bro. James Foulhouze resigned his membership in the ex-S.C., because III. Bro. Charles Claibome, 33d had ridiculed his costumes, his masonic frocks.* Lamarre. *A Masonic Trial in New Orleans - May 22, 1858* (New Orleans: J. Lamarre, 1858) 24. It seems unthinkable that this could have been the sole reason for Foulhouze resigning his office in the

Supreme Council of Louisiana, but it is an interesting look at the volatile atmosphere.

54 Folger, *Ancient and Accepted Scottish Rite, 312-314.*

55. 18 November 1856. Harris/Carter, *History,* 252.

56. Albert Mackey wrote to Ladebat on 27 February 1859 informing him of his election. Ladebat wrote back to Mackey on 19 March accepting the office and, interestingly, expressed a desire for a supreme council to be established in each state. Ibid., 266.

57. Following the 1850 *Constitution of the Grand Lodge of Louisiana,* the French Rite was not accommodated by the Grand Lodge. With no superior body for the government of the French Rite Lodges, they eventually lost their identity and their unique nature. An attempt was made in the late 1800's to revive the French Rite in New Orleans through the short-lived Grand Orient of Louisiana (French or Modern Rite). This body was created in 1879 but, possibly due to little support, did not last longer than 10 years. See: *The Grand Orient of Louisiana: A Short History and Catechism of a Lost French Rite Masonic Body,* Introduction by Michael R. Poll (New Orleans: Cornerstone Book Publishers, 2008 reprint of 1886 edition).

58. On 7 October 1856, James Foulhouze and the other former officers of the Supreme Council of Louisiana who resigned in 1853 announced that the body had never ceased to exist. The New Orleans Council (under Foulhouze) and the Charleston Council (under Pike) engaged in bitter attacks. For presently unknown reasons, Foulhouze abandoned the Supreme Council of Louisiana in the mid 1860's.

59. Samory would return to New Orleans and die there on 30 July 1889 and Ladebat would remain in France and die there on 22 December 1882.

60. Charles Laffon de Ladebat to Albert Pike June 24, 1860. Original in the Archives of the Supreme Council Southern Jurisdiction USA. Photocopy in possession of this author.

The Origin and Nature of Freemasonry
By Clayton J. "Chip" Borne, III, PGM

Freemasonry in particular its origin and nature are topics of intense debate among Masonic historians. Their positions are supported by diverse historical, sociological, economic and religious theories. Some of these persuasions are tendered with compelling evidence however others are offered as educated speculation.

The Genesis of Speculative Freemasonry is found primarily in the operational reflection attributed to the craft guilds and their development in the Art of building. From the early stone masons, progress is seen in the records of the magnificent medieval construction of Castles, Cathedrals and Monasteries. The Primitive craft with its skills and architectural genius combined with their spiritual objectives, clearly became the model for Modern or Speculative Freemasonry. Some of the more popular hypothesis as to the Craft's origin originate with the following:

The most universally accepted Legend is the Temple Theory which centered around the building of King Solomon's Temple in 1200 BC, with King Solomon's charges being received from his father, David, and imparted to his artisan craftsman. An interesting contrast is the Prestonian Theory, which discounts the Temple Theory and has the fraternity emerging at the time of Julius Caesar's invasion of the British Isles in 55 BC and perpetuated by Carrausius, Admiral of the Roman Navy, at York, 290 AD. The Anderson Theory which also abandons the traditional Temple Theory develops a legendary account from the Bible, with the Moral Sciences being taught by Adam to two of his sons, Cain and Seth, and further passed down to Noah's descendants who in 3000 BC were the builders of the Tower of Babel. The Hutchinson Theory states our Masonic fraternity is based on the Patriotical and Mosaic dispensation or periods of scriptures. It was tendered further to successive generations with the Master Degree emblematical of the Christian dispensation. The Oliverian Theory was the creation of Reverend Oliver, a learned Anglican clergyman who embraced the traditional legend of the Craft and asserts further that the philosophy of Freemasonry actually existed in principle before the creation of the universe, with Adam having been taught the Moral Sciences by God. The Ramsey Theory stated that the Legend of the Craft did not arise out of humble architectural or operative craft but from the very elite of Medieval Society, namely the Crusaders known as the Knights Templars returning from the battle fields of Palestine. The Pike Theory asserts the Craft's origin is found in the moral disciplines of the Ancient Mysteries.

Having no canonical order to confirm and define Freemasonry's origin, existing evidence supports three distinct identities. There is one identity which reflects Scotland's traditions, one of England's thought and one of Ireland's customs, resulting in a unique diversity of the Order. The most interesting inquiry by this writer was to search for a consistency which was common to all three. The common factor is that each comprises the history of mankind supported by a moral philosophy whose ancestral beginnings are first reflected in certain dynamic Ancient Societies. This belief or school of thought has a rich past with its early Artisan ancestry surfacing as being identifiable in the operative Craft Societies and Guilds of the Middle Ages. Those Guilds and their defining principles can be traced to and found historically in the Charges or Moral Codes of the Ancient Societies. The original text of those ancient Charges appears later in certain 18th Century manuscripts.

The Ancient Manuscripts contain explicit moral standards referred to as Old Charges or disciplines. The documents usually begin with a prayer followed by a history of the Craft. The introduction was followed by the Ancient principles or charges which were implemented to define social civility and the implement the administration of Justice. The documents end with an oath and closing prayer. The text of most of these documents are explicitly Christian with fraternal parameters such as mandating obedience to God, respect for the master and members of the lodges and addressed personal conduct. They also mandate fraternal instruction such as to bury the dead, support widows, etc. They present conclusive evidence establishing a true standard which was maintained by these societies from the earliest of time. As a philosophy of life, the Old Charges are the chief documentary evidence for links between the medieval stonemasons and the enlightenment of Modern Freemasonry. It was upon these principles that dynamic civilization, such as the Early Greek and Roman Empires were established. Masonry's philosophical history has been described by its Historians as Ancient or Primitive Masonry.

Schools of Research as an overview, the diverse theories as to our Craft's historical origin, have been researched and crafted by distinguished Masonic Historians into five major schools of Academic Research: Authentic (Study of Historical Documents), Anthropological (Study of the Craft Labors of Ancient Man), Sociological (Study of Man as a Social Creature), Mystical (Study of Hermetic Spiritual Disciplines), and Occultic (Study of Early Chemistry and the Natural Sciences). As this thesis develops, examples of each school will be evident.

The Mystical School forms a most interesting study as to what some believe to be the identity and object of Freemasonry. It states that each member's hermetic rebirth resides in the attainment of gnostic spiritual knowledge which will free the mind from the bounds of a material prescription or existence.

The Occultic School reflects the study of early chemistry and natural sciences and promotes the evolution of spiritual evolution and advancement through a system of esoteric knowledge its methodology is responsible for the creation of early medicines and later medical schools.

The Sociological School examines the development, structure and inner personal relations functioning within human society.

The Authentic School is most prevalent as it is based on a study of actual historical documents. The absence of written history of the craft prior to the discovery of the Regius or Halliwell Manuscript, of 1390, the oldest and most comprehensive researchable Masonic document, which references the first recorded Grand Lodge meetings in York, England, in 600 and 925 AD, which limits the Authentic School and mandates that we revert our research prior to that time to a sociological and comparative study of the history of Government, Religion, Art and Architecture, in order to examine the only reliable evidence of the ancient core movement which culminated in our present-day Brotherhood.

The earliest written reference to craft masonry was the Work of a Chaldean Priest/Historian, Berosus, writing around 2000 BC whose insights into Babylonia and Assyria 's culture and history were revealing. In his writings, he replicates the history of an unnamed Sumerian historian writing circa 4200 BC relating the conditions following the Great Flood (Noah's Flood) and the Revelation of the Two Pillars of Stone or Columns on which were written the Sciences. He writes of Hermenes, who later is called "Hermes". The writings reflect the building of the Tower of Babylon, i.e., "Babel" and there was the Craft of Masonry made much of and the King of Babylon who was called Hembroth, who was a mason and loved well the Craft. The King passed the knowledge of the Two Pillars to sixty masons who were sent into Egypt where Abraham and Sarah, his wife, along with an ingenious scholar called Euclid taught the sciences to the sons of the Egyptian King. He further states that at the building of the Temple of Babel there was masons of much esteem. Euclid taught the princes that they should live well together, be loyal to the Pharaoh and the Lords they served and be true to one another. And call one another fellow and not servant or other names and serve for their payment to the Lords they serve. This evidence has given additional creditability as this ancient historian, Berosus' account is also recorded in the 926 *Reqius Manuscript* and the Book of Genesis found in the Old Testament of the King James Bible.

Many respected modern-day historians have challenged the issue of the origin and meaning of Speculative Freemasonry which academic journeys as we have stated traditionally begin attempting to prove whether or not the Craft began in England, Ireland, Scotland or an Ancient Migration from Europe. Some of the more compelling theories, however are referenced as follows: Gould and Hughan's Enigmatic Theory, Koop and Jones's Transition Theory, Robert's, Secret Society Theory; Yates, Rosicrucian Theory; Margaret Jacobs, Transition Enlightenment Theory; Stevenson's, Scottish Origin Theory; Harry Carr's, Transition Theory; and Berman's Speculative/Spiritual Theory. As a historian, my view is similar to the Jacobs Theory as I believe that position is more reflective of relevant historical events. Each Theory, however, becomes a study in itself as each formulates a theoretical position as to the Crafts Origin. Two major academic theories or practices have emerged. One opposing theory to the mainstream of thought is as follows:

> *"There is still today no reliable proof that Modern Day Freemasonry originated from the Mid Evil Corporations of Cathedral Builders, consequently the "Accepted Freemason" is a movement established in England, free and independent of the Corporations or Guilds, earlier than the seventeenth century, which encompassed the Old English Operative Traditions and Duties."* (Birth of Freemasonry by Eric Ward)

The academic approaches are identified as the "Traditional" and the "Transitional" schools. When we speak of Tradition, we are referring to a classical principle such as a metaphysical truth or finite doctrine which has traversed the history of time such as the democratic principles of Greece and Rome that are reflected in the Constitution of the United States and its Bill of Rights. It is a truth that is transmitted with the aim of being preserved. When we speak of "Transition" it postures a position that Modern Masonry is merely a morphing of the Ancient principles which adapted only to function in a Modern Society.

The diverse theories are evident in the *decisions* of the United States Supreme Court. The Conservative Justices such as Honorable Clarence Thomas are Traditionalist dedicated to preserving democratic principles of the Constitution and Bill of Rights and believe that what its writers achieved remains just as relevant and modern and up to date as when it was written in 1787. The Transitionalist views are reflected in the decision of the Liberal Justices who reflect a very different reading of the Constitution, as it relates to the Civility of Modern Society in that they want a document that evolves by judicial ruling.

The Code of Freemasonry, in this Author's opinion, is seen as metaphysical truths that were preserved over the centuries by certain societies during the *Age of Enlightenment*, (1685 to approximately 1815) resulting in an atmosphere of free though unrestrained by the Church or the Monarchy so as to freely and openly embrace their liberating concepts. These philosophies are expressed in the writings of such as philosophers such as Bacon (Hermetic Tradition), Hobbs (Social Contact Theory: Desire and Fear), Descarte (Concepts of Analytical Geometry Math/Science: The Authority of Reason "I think therefore I am") and Locke (Doctrine of Liberalism/Republicanism/Mystical Separation of Church and State). These liberating concepts were the catalyst for such social reforms as the American and French Revolutions, which were fostered and encouraged by the developing history of Freemasonry. The Concepts of Federalism are found in the 1723 Anderson Constitution. Those Federalist ideas are principles of Freemasonry. To honor and keep those defining fundamental principles is to enrich the democratic concepts of the founding fathers many of whom were Freemasons.

The Moral Code of these dynamic leaders preserved over time certain fundamental human behavioral disciplines which are found recorded in the early manuscripts and referred to by Masonic historians as the Ancient Charges. They begin with the concept of Monotheism or a belief in the oneness of a Creator. In general, the Charges go further in addressing the concepts of Immorality, Brotherly Love, Honesty, Secrecy, Fidelity, Trust, Equality, Morality, Conduct, Self Esteem, Learning and others. The evidence in support of these disciplines are found in Ancient Documents such as the Regius, or Halliwell Manuscript which document is compelling evidence of the first documents Grand Lodge in 926 AD at York, England. Many of these Disciplines or Charges recorded in this and other Ancient Manuscripts became the principles accepted today as the "Landmarks of Freemasonry".

Although, the Freemason Code is spiritual in nature, Freemasonry is not, nor has it ever been a religion because by definition it does not delineate or impose on its members the most fundamental criteria of a religion which is a defined plan or means to salvation. The craft accepts and respects all religions and encourages active participation, however from the earliest of times require only that a man adhere to the belief in a Supreme Being as prerequisite for membership.

Monotheism being the human acceptance and belief in the concept of the oneness of God was slow to gain favor in Ancient Societies. It embodies the aspiration of the soul toward the absolute and infinite intelligence, namely the one Supreme Deity, God. It was gradual, with the people unwilling to relinquish their guardian deities: Diana, Zeus, Apollo, Hermes, and the most cherished Demeter "Mother Earth" and her daughter, Persephone. The motivation was the mystery of Transubstantiation which is emblematical of the spirit life after death and to the desire to eventually, upon death, be transformed or to pass to it. It advocates a personal Transformation, or the development of a character that recognizes the need to subrogate self-interest to the interest of the common welfare.

The basic disciplines of life today as in ancient times have embraced and centered around the essential social precepts of Truth, the concepts of Justice and the fundamentals of Liberty. Our Order is neither religious nor political but encourages each member to actively pursue his religion of choice and be peacefully involved with his government. The Discipline of Ancient or Primitive Masonry actively advocated a spiritual awareness for improving one's self and a true concern for our fellow man. The discipline, which can be seen in the various aspects of human development, matures by virtue of a transformation into a kinder and humbler attitude by the Brotherhood and collectively transforms a maturing society. Its reflection in government, religion, art and architecture evidences and confirms its existence.

Conclusion: Modern Freemasonry is a phenomenon that has appeared relevant to so many diverse people for hundreds of years. The Order parallels life, in its principles, symbolism, formation and development. It is therefore a philosophical progressive science built upon the traditions and core foundational disciplines of its predecessors. It is the oldest initiatory society in the world of today which is not dependent on a governmental or religious institution for its survival. Despite its emphasis on regularity in the maintenance of its standards, the issues of traditions, transmissions and authority are now dogmatic in the sense that its ritual, symbols and practices are defined within each particular jurisdiction of which there are hundreds of lodges with whom we are in amenity. Fundamental to the crafts development is the understanding of the evidence that was found in the medieval stone mason's guilds spiritual disciplines now refer to as the "Old Charges". They are clearly stated in of the most popular Reguis and Cook Manuscripts which set forth the fundamental parameters of civility and the conduct required in human relationships. It is this ancient standard or moral code that is seen by this author as a Philosophy of Life and forms the basis for the international appeal of Freemasonry.

The historical importance of the Institution of Freemasonry and its influence on the development of humanity irrespective of its origin in this writer's opinion is found reflected in the mysteries of the Orders Ritual which was developed within the security of its tiled Lodges. From the earliest of time, however the uniqueness of the structure of the Lodges afforded its members an academic environment where the Brotherhood were able to discuss the Secret Art of their trade. More importantly than their trade however, the craftsman was free to think and reason about important philosophical issues that   affected society not possible in the enforced orthodoxy, restricted by the Monarchy and the Church. Masonry did not have an official voice.

Freedom of thought, however, was basic to the order. The early developing craft guilds were the prime movers and dynamic catalyst for the defense of human dignity and human rights. The sociological evolution and its disciplines were brought to life during the Age of Enlightenment of the 18th Century. It resulted in a society or Brotherhood that stands in opposition to any civilization that has lost its spiritual and metaphysical values.

Bibliography

Hutchins: *Pillars of Wisdom*, Revised, 1995, Pg.9

Berman, Rick: *The Schism*, Sussex Academic Press 2013, Pg. 186-187

Gan, Richard: *The Treasures of English Freemasonry 1717 to 2017*

Bogdam and Shoek: *Handbook of Freemasonry*, Prescott Ed. Ch. 2 & 3, 2014

Pike, Albert: *The Meaning of Freemasonry*, 1924, MSA, Pg. 32, 33, 36 & 37

Leadbeater, C.W.: *Freemasonry and its Ancient Mystic Rites,* Theosophical Pub. House, 1986
Chassagnard: *From Stonemason to Freemason,* Prescott Ed. 2013, Pg. 41 & 47
Farlo, Venzi: *Studies on Traditional Freemasonry,* 2012, Ch 1, Pg. 24, 25, 207, Rev. 6-1-14

Masonic Ritual in the United States
By Michael R. Poll

In the United States, there is, for the most part, one accepted craft ritual. It is the ritual, or a version of it, that is worked in the vast majority of the lodges. It is the ritual hammered out by Thomas Smith Webb in the late 1700's. It's known, unofficially, as the "Webb Ritual"; the "Preston / Webb Ritual" and even "the American Rite." But in most cases, it is simply known, in the U.S. as, "the craft ritual." It is most often called by no name, because a name is not really necessary.

Maybe to better understand the situation, think of a small town where there is only one grocery. The grocery will certainly have a name. It may be named "The Central Grocery," or "Joe's Grocery," or whatever name they gave it. But the point is that because there is only one grocery in that town, they can just call it "the grocery." "I'm going to the grocery." Sure, if there were more than one grocery, they have to identify which grocery, like, "I'm going to Joe's Grocery."

This is the same situation that exists in most areas of U.S. Masonry. When we, in the U.S., talk of the craft lodge, we are almost always talking about one ritual and one rite. Further identification is not needed.

Sure, by now, many have heard about those 10 Scottish Rite craft lodges under the jurisdiction of the Grand Lodge of Louisiana. But it's a big country, and most everywhere else there is just one ritual.

In his paper, "The Webb Ritual in the United States,"[1] Silas Shepherd tells us of the Masons involved in the development of what would become the ritual used by most all of Masonry in the United States. It is an interesting story and provides details on not only the Webb ritual but the other players and events which had a role in the ritual's development.

It would seem that just following the American War of Independence, Freemasonry in the United States went through something of an identity crisis. The lodges and provincial Grand lodges in the new country were cut off from their mother bodies, mostly in the United Kingdom. There was a period of time when it was not certain what would happen with Masonry in the youthful United States of America.

Some felt that maybe there should be one Grand Lodge for the entire country. Suggestions were made that maybe even George Washington should become the first Grand Master. Others felt that if the states were to be truly important pieces in a whole, and that the country was based on the collective authority of the states, then maybe each state should have a sovereign and independent Grand Lodge.

When the debates were over, the new county settled on the concept of one Grand Lodge per state, but they also agreed, in theory, on one ritual per state and the suggestion that they should be one language, and that would be English. The idea for Masonry in the United States would seem to be that it was desirous for every state to be independent, but a copy of the other. It would seem that to be like others was good and to be unlike the rest was not good. Over time this concept did create problems.

One problem was that everyone was not alike. Just to give one example, in 1803, the young United States grew in size by almost a third when it obtained from France the massive section of land known as the Louisiana purchase. At the heart of this purchase was the important port of New Orleans. But this was a French territory with most of the citizens speaking French, and proud to be of French heritage.

Masonry, as best as we can tell, had existed in New Orleans since 1752. It's nature and language matched its members, meaning French. As English speaking, American Masons arrived in the area, they found the Masonry in New Orleans different than that in the rest of the U.S. It became a problem for them and resulted in Masonic conflict for many years to follow. But, since we know that more than one Masonic ritual exists in the world, does it help, hurt or not matter at all if we limit our lodges to only one ritual? In my opinion, and from the standpoint of initiation, it doesn't matter at all. The differences in rituals are all a matter of choice, a matter of preference or even just what is available in the area. At best, it's all a matter of taste.

The various rituals may have different words, actions and even different feels to them, but at the heart of them all is the Hiramic legend. It is that legend and the symbolic teachings woven into it that defines a Masonic initiation from other forms of initiation.

An initiation is not considered valid because it was done using the words of this or that ritual. An initiation is valid when it reaches in and touches the candidate deep within. Any of the Masonic rites are capable of doing that, or not doing it. Problems for lodges come not because they are practicing different rituals, but because they are not performing valid initiations.

But in reality, even with the claims of many that there is one craft ritual in the United States, over time these rituals have changed from jurisdiction to jurisdiction. Some variations in ritual are small and some large. It is far more likely that Masonic craft rituals are identical to each other within a jurisdiction than from jurisdiction to jurisdiction. It is because of the fact that jurisdictions are sovereign and independent that they have independently, and over time, made changes to their own ritual. These changes are often unique to their jurisdiction.

The 1700s and early 1800s were creative times in Freemasonry. During the time when the Webb Ritual would become the ritual for the bulk of U.S. Masonry, there were many beautiful systems of Freemasonry created around the world. In many areas, multiple rituals worked side-by-side reflecting the rich nature of Masonic initiation. The enlightened do not view one ritual as better or superior to another, but only as a different path to reach the same destination.

The fact that Masonry in the United States does not utilize all of the different rituals, can be viewed as a missed opportunity for variety in lodge meetings, but really, in itself, that is only a minor inconvenience.

On the other hand, there is a misunderstanding, or a lack of understanding, concerning the nature of the Masonic Rites. This misunderstanding may exist because of the way that Freemasonry developed in the United States.

The two Masonic Rites which are dominant in the United States are the York Rite and the Scottish Rite. The Scottish Rite, or more correctly, the Ancient and Accepted Scottish Rite, is a 33-degree Masonic system. It was created in 1801 in Charleston, South Carolina. The rituals used by this Rite come from older systems and rituals mainly from France. The other major Masonic Rite in the U.S. is commonly known as the "York Rite" and concludes with the degree of Knight Templar. Sometimes also known as the "American Rite" it was hammered out around the same time that Webb was working on his craft rituals.

Albert Mackey used the term "American Rite" rather than "York Rite" as he felt the system was distinctly an American creation and to avoid confusion with systems and degrees of like name in England. Mackey was not successful in changing the official name of the rite and "York Rite" has become the popular and accepted name.

Because of the popularity of the two high degree Masonic systems that have survived in the U.S., and the desire for there to be only one craft ritual, a possibly unforeseen problem has developed. The problem when looked at from a Masonic ritualistic standpoint is that for something to be a Masonic Rite, it must begin in the craft lodge and then conclude at whatever final degree exists for that Rite. The first degree of any Masonic Rite must be the Entered Apprentice Degree

The situation for the United States, on first notice, is that we have two high grade Masonic Rites that appear to begin *after* the Master Mason degree and then continue on to the completion of this system. Most Masons in the United States pay little attention to the degree progression and simply accept that the Masonic rites, the high-grade bodies, begin *after* the craft Lodge degrees. They appear separate and independent from craft Lodge Masonry.

Let's look at this situation. A good illustration for this discussion is an old Masonic print titled "The Steps of Freemasonry."

I find this piece of art very interesting and what I like about this particular piece of artwork is not that it portrays the actual nature of the Scottish Rite and the York Rite, but that it portrays how Freemasonry is worked from an organizational standpoint in the United States. I'd like to take a moment to examine this art and see exactly what is telling us as to how we view the Masonic rites.

The artwork is created along the lines of a pyramid with a base and then two sets of steps going up each side of the pyramid. If you look on the side labeled the Scottish Rite, it shows a step for each of the degrees and finally the degree of Sovereign Grand Inspector General, which is the 33rd and last degree. On the York Rite side, it also shows steps along with figures representing each of degrees of the York Rite concluding with its final step, the degree of Knight Templar. Also, if you look in the center area of the pyramid there is an arch, and inside of the arch there are a number of little figures which represent different organizations. This grouping of figures is identified as Allied Organizations. This collection is composed of organizations such as the Shrine, Grotto, the Eastern Star and other Allied Organizations. These organizations are outside of the craft lodge or, outside of the actual rites of Freemasonry.

At the very bottom of the artwork you see three steps which provide the foundation for the whole pyramid. These three steps represent the craft lodge and the degrees of Entered Apprentice, Fellowcraft, and Master Mason. You see here a number of figures ascending up these steps. If you follow their directions, they go to the steps of the Scottish

Rite or to the steps of the York Rite. The illusion and message that is given is that you have three separate set of steps available. There is the craft lodge steps, the steps of the Scottish Rite and the steps of the York Rite.

The Allied Organizations are a bit higher up the steps and the suggestion is that once you have received your Master Mason degree, you can apply to these bodies. The Shrine is set higher up on steps in this section as, for many years, in order to join the Shrine, you would either have to be a 32nd degree Scottish Rite Mason or a Knight Templar in the York Rite. This prerequisite has changed, and one needs only have received the Master Mason degree to become a Shriner today.

Now, if you take the Allied Organizations out of consideration and away from the image, you are left with the steps for the Scottish Rite, the York Rite and the craft lodge degrees. The art seems to be suggesting that you have three separate entities. Since the craft lodge serves as the foundation piece, then once you have completed the steps of the craft lodge, you can then advance to the steps of the Scottish Rite or York Rite. The fact is that the Scottish Rite and the York Rite are both complete systems of Masonry with their own unique craft lodges. This artwork creates a misunderstanding as to the nature of a Masonic Rite. Both the York Rite and the Scottish Rite begin their degree structure, or steps, in the Entered Apprentice degree. What is *not* delivered in this piece of art is that both the Scottish Rite as well as the York Rite have their own unique craft lodge rituals. All that is represented is *the* craft Lodge. So, you don't realize that instead of two set of steps with a common foundation in the craft lodge, it should be two complete set of steps, each with their own individual craft lodge steps. Neither the Scottish Rite nor the York Rite begin their degrees *after* the Master Mason degree. The Scottish Rite and York Rite begin their systems in the own unique craft rituals.

In the New Orleans area, there are 10 lodges working under the jurisdiction of the Grand Lodge of Louisiana which work in the Ancient and Accepted Scottish Rite craft Lodge ritual. This is the actual first 3 degrees of the Scottish Rite or otherwise known as the Scottish Rite blue Lodge degrees.

As a side note, the Scottish Rite craft lodges in the New Orleans area have never been known by the term "Red Lodge". The term "Red Lodge" began and has been used in various places around the world to refer to Scottish Rite craft lodges. But not New Orleans.

Regardless of how the poster "The Steps of Freemasonry" illustrates the nature of Freemasonry, The York Rite and the Scottish Rite each have their own unique foundational or craft Lodge ritual. The foundational or craft Lodge ritual for the York Rite is the ritual used in most all craft lodges in the United States. The foundational or craft Lodge ritual for the Scottish Rite is limited, with rare exception, to the rituals used by the 10 lodges under the jurisdiction of the Grand Lodge of Louisiana. These 10 lodges comprise the 16th Masonic District of the Grand Lodge of Louisiana. In other areas of the world, however, the Scottish Rite craft ritual is one of the most popular of craft lodge rituals.

I believe the best way to understand the quite easy to misunderstand nature of the American Masonic rites is to look at the early days of masonry in the United States.

Because of the early desire of the Masons in the new United States of America to have one Grand Lodge per state as well as one ritual per state it created a situation which made it impossible to have approved multiple rituals worked in any of the jurisdictions.

When the 33 degree Ancient and Accepted Scottish Rite was created in 1801 in Charleston, South Carolina, a difficult situation already existed in that state. Without getting into a complex history of Masonry in England, there were two Grand lodges in South Carolina which traced their roots to English Masonry, but different styles of English Masonry.

I would recommend additional reading on the early history of English Freemasonry regarding the Ancients and the Moderns. These two Masonic philosophies resulted in two competing Grand Lodges in England, one commonly known as the Moderns and the other the Ancients. In 1813, they overcame their differences and join together to create the United Grand Lodge of England.

In South Carolina in 1801, each of these English style Grand Lodges existed in the state.

This presented problems to the rest of the U.S. Grand Lodges because of their desire to have only one Grand Lodge per state. On the surface, both of these Grand Lodges in South Carolina seemed perfectly regular and the desire for the balance of U.S. Freemasonry was for these two bodies to merge into one. The problem was that the members of these two Grand lodges had a strong dislike of each other. They did not want to merge as each believed their own Grand Lodge possessed the correct Masonic philosophy.

Because of the problems created by these two Grand lodges and their resistance to merge, it created an impossible situation for the Ancient and Accepted Scottish Rite when it was created in Charleston in 1801.

Simply put, the idea of a third body, the supreme council, controlling craft lodges in that state was unthinkable. The two Grand lodges in South Carolina did eventually put aside their differences, merge and become the Grand Lodge of South Carolina.

The Scottish Rite apparently traded their craft lodges for existence and only worked as an organization from the fourth degree onward. By doing this, the U.S. Masonic community could maintain their desire for one Grand Lodge and one ritual approved in each state.

In Louisiana, and while these 10 lodges working in the Scottish Rite ritual are under the jurisdiction of the Grand Lodge, the simple fact that more than one ritual existed created great problems in Louisiana Masonry in the mid-1800s.

The desire for one Grand Lodge and one ritual nearly tore Masonry apart in the state. This one Grand Lodge and one ritual per state concept also created a misunderstanding about Masonic rites themselves.

As shown in the poster, the craft Lodge became almost a separate entity rather than the foundational degrees of our Masonic rites.

A Masonic ritual is simply the vehicle used to deliver a Masonic initiation. If it were a play, it would be the script. A Masonic Rite is a particular type of ritual and all of the degrees that are associated with it. Throughout history there have been many different Masonic rites and rituals. Each of the historic Masonic rituals and rites have their own unique beauty and manner of symbolic instruction.

In the early history of Masonry in the United States, we did have more Masonic rites than we do today. The Order of the Royal Secret, the French or Modern Rite and the Egyptian Rite of Memphis are just a few of the Rites once worked in the United States.

While the creative time in our Masonic history, when new Rites and rituals were commonplace, seems to have passed, who knows what tomorrow will bring ?For all I know, a new wave of Masonic rites and rituals could be in our future. If there is one thing of which I'm certain it is that no matter what we have today it will at some point change.

Notes:

1. Shepherd, Silas. "The Webb Ritual in the United States." *Masonic Enlightenment: The Philosophy, History and Wisdom of Freemasonry.* Ed. Michael R. Poll. New Orleans, LA: Cornerstone Book Publishers, 2006. pp 10-17.

Seeing Through the Eyes of the Blind
By Jonathan K. Poll

It is a fundamental aspect of Freemasonry that each of us is seeking light. What this means is for each of us to determine, but once Masonry has opened our eyes to its truths, you begin to see its teachings play out in our everyday lives. It was just before a college class that I was asked a question that strongly invoked this fundamental aspect of our teachings. One of my classmates, who was born totally blind, asked me what it was like to see. I was caught completely off guard. I had a little exposure to this subject, but his question still hit me totally out of left field. The only response that I could muster in the moment was that having always been sighted I didn't really know how to describe it. To this day, I'm not satisfied with my response. I have often thought back and wondered what better answer I could have given him. How could I even tackle something as large as describing such a pivotal sense to someone with no point of reference? I turned it over in my head again and again. While I never again had the opportunity to properly answer my classmate directly, I gave a lot of thought to what I would've liked to say and how the answer helped me better relate to the world around me.

If I were to try and explain sight to my classmate, what I would need to do is bridge my experience with theirs using something with which they are familiar with. I could use sound as an anchor point. Sound, I suppose, would be an extremely significant part of my classmate's life. If you consider them together there seems to be similarities between sight and sound. There is often a relationship between what an object looks like and what it sounds like. A metal ball, for example, will make a different sound when tapped on a table than a rubber ball. On a more scientific level, another similarity is that while the ear detects vibrations traveling through the air, the eyes are detecting light particles (or waves depending on the light's mood) that are reflecting off of objects. Both senses are interacting with outside forces as those forces interact with the world around us. One analogy for sight could be it is like *hearing* silent sound. It is as though seeing is the act of hearing a quiet noise given off by every object all the time. Just as the ears 'hear' the result of an action traveling through the air, the eyes 'hear' silent sounds that emanate from the reflection of energy from a light source as it interacts with everything around us. Because the ears only 'hear' when there is an interaction between objects, and the eyes 'hear' nearly constantly so long as there is an adequate light source, it would appear that sight is a far more perceptive sense than hearing. However, it would seem the limitations of sight are far sharper.

One of my classmate's remarks on this subject is that he didn't understand how a sighted person *couldn't* see something. If, for example, a sighted person dropped a pencil, how could they not instantly see it and retrieve it. I would suppose he is using sound as a reference point here, because if a chair tipped over in a room, it would be very hard for him not to hear it. However, it is much easier not to see something than it is not to hear it. Sounds can be more easily heard if they are in front of you or to your sides and are somewhat harder to hear if they are behind you. Whereas sound has this soft limitation, sight has an absolute one. There is no seeing what is behind you without manual intervention, as someone could no more see out of the back of their head than my classmate could see at all. A sighted person could compensate for their limited field of vison by moving their eyes, head, or entire body to search for an errant pencil. This is not dissimilar from cupping your hand around your ear to hear better or moving to a closer location. You can even draw even further comparisons like, just as doors and walls make listening through difficult, sight with its sharper limitations makes seeing through most objects impossible. By examining the basics of sight, bit by bit, a foundation is laid to bridge my classmate's world to abstract concepts like the nature of seeing.

Explaining these basic principles of sight might make some people cringe. Surely endeavoring to do something as hopeless as explaining sight to the blind is at best condescending and at worst mockery. However, taking such a position misses the point entirely. For one explaining aspects of reality is not only for the benefit of the blind individual but for the sighted person as well. How often would the average man be prompted to examine something as intuitive and fundamental as seeing. By explaining something to someone who has no point of reference, especially such a fundamental sense, is a deep expression of empathy. You have to mentally delve into their head, envision how they perceive the world, and form a strategy to connect their world of experience with yours. Even if a blind man is never to see, having the knowledge of what sight is could help him better relate to his seeing brethren. In answering these seemingly basic questions, we are called to face and examine fundamental aspects of our lives and examine them through the eyes of another. What else would give us cause to explore something as basic as seeing if not for the innocent curiosity of someone who can't.

This exercise caused me to consider those who could be considered *blind* in an entirely different manner. If someone's mental, emotional, or philosophical disposition is as alien to me as being without sight is, it would be too easy to disregard them as ignorant, bigoted, or any other unpleasant adjective. Describing basic concepts as kindness, empathy, or selflessness to someone who regards these virtues contemptuously might seem as ridiculous as describing to a blind man what it is to see. But is it ridiculous? It *would* be ridiculous if I were to preach down to them about how to be a good functioning member of society. Instead, if I were to truly learn their philosophies, find an anchor point, and build a bridge to explain my reality to them through their own, I could forge a connection to them where none existed before. Just as teaching about sight to the blind must be done with care so as not to become condescending, so is it as critical to be on the level with someone whose views might dramatically differ from mine. Sometimes someone whose beliefs and actions are so different from ours can cause feelings of anger and revulsion to emerge. I fear these types of emotions are the genesis for many of the ills that are plaguing our society now.

I am not suggesting taking steps to covert those who disagree with you to your cause. That could be as impossible as teaching a blind man about seeing in the hopes it will endow him with sight. I do believe, however, taking the time to build bridges with those who starkly disagree with you could enrich both your lives. You might ease the fire of hatred in someone's heart and replace fear with camaraderie. Just as delving into something as simple as sight could be deeply rewarding, imagine the bounty that could be obtained by exploring something as fundamental as virtue. The very act could give you a deeper understanding of your own beliefs, while also helping someone who could be in dire need of a friendly hand.

If we believe that those who differ from us, however, are somehow morally depraved, and underserving of such consideration then the need to reexamine our own beliefs becomes all that more dire. It wasn't that long ago that we as a people felt that way of the physically blind. We thought that they had offended God in some manner so that they were at fault for their perceived affliction. There is also the unspoken fear that having to examine and lay bare our ideas of virtue and our inner philosophies could leave us vulnerable. After all, there are a considerable number of the human race who feel virtue is a weakness to be repressed and shunned. What if this examination proves them correct? What I say to this is that an honest and open examination of inner virtue could no more diminish it, than an examination of sight could render you blind. If you find your philosophies wanting, then there is always room to improve. It helps me greatly not to view what I believe as who I am but tools that I carry with me. I truly believe it is the fear of loss that keeps so many at bay from understanding and relating with each other.

I wish I had thought through a better answer for my classmate before he ever asked that question. Maybe I would have made a dear friend rather than a passing acquaintance. I will, however, carry with me the lessons that encounter taught me. This experience has given me a new understanding for our Masonic search for light. Not just in interacting with the physically blind but also those who are philosophically alien to me. Our Masonic teachings leads us to a path of forging deeper connections to all our neighbors throughout the world. Learning how they perceive the world without judging them or censoring them and using how they see the world to bridge the divide. Through these metaphysical bridges, we could unite and enrich our lives far better than if all our thoughts and ideas were melted down into a homogenous slurry. Even if the blind does indeed never see as we do, maybe they never needed to. The blind and the seeing could instead show each other perspectives that neither considered nor had the capability to see before. Through a mutual understanding, we broaden all our horizons and knit this human family closer together.

The Importance of the EA Degree in Understanding Our World as a Master Mason
By J. Quincy Gotte

I recall how I felt after being raised a Master Mason. I was excited to learn all there was to know about Freemasonry, and couldn't wait to receive my first lesson as a Master Mason. But I must confess that even as the MM Degree, with all its drama and symbolic allegories, is presented as the apex of the Freemason's journey, the EA Degree still fascinates me. Ever since I was raised a Master Mason, I've always walked with the EA Degree close beside me. There were times that I wondered if I was really a Master Mason. I mean, we all know what makes us a Master Mason, and I guess I'm as much a Master Mason as the next by those terms. But to be truthful and honest, because I don't always feel as though I've mastered myself or even fully understand how to, a part of me still feels like I am an Entered Apprentice Mason. I used to be troubled by these feelings, and couldn't put my finger on why a part of me felt compelled to be ashamed of feeling like an Entered Apprentice, and a part of me was completely ok with it and excited to be one, or at least feel like one. So, I decided to devote some thought in understanding more clearly as to how a Master Mason can still feel like an Entered Apprentice Mason, and why one would feel compelled to under value the position of an Entered Apprentice Mason.

As I pondered and studied, and became more pensive; I realized that this is not off base at all with "The Great Aim" of Freemasonry, which will be alluded to going forward. As a matter of thought, I believe it is safe to say that most Master Masons feel as though they are still an Entered Apprentice Mason at times-- and rightfully so; after all, the Entered Apprentice Degree is all about coming to a realization about our rudimentary connection to this wondrous imperfect world by which we are bound to

80

throughout our entire lives, and how we must work with our disassembling elements and build a perfect Temple.

The City and the Tower

The realization of our base nature and its continuance is indispensable to our work as Master Masons. So as a Mason, there is value in our base nature and its connection to this imperfect world. Striving to rise above this world and become or return to something much greater is naturally instilled within our being. This raw ambition, which is so much a part of mankind, is what employs our actions and enables us to achieve extraordinary feats. We can read in the book of Genesis a story about the building of the Tower of Babel. It tells us how the people of that city worked together in one accord to build a tower so that they could elevate their physical status to align with how they viewed themselves to be. Now there are many lessons to be learned in this story which range anywhere from communication of mankind to a contrast of the New Jerusalem spoken of in St. John's Apocalypse. But ultimately, this story teaches that success was not realized by the manner in which their ambition was employed. I prefer to view the story of Nimrod's city as displaying man's efforts to rise above himself, climbing and striving to obtain the Holiness that is beyond his grasp; using a tower or temple built by his own physical hand driven by his ill-applied ambition. Nimrod's city is a perfect picture of man's base nature at work and its failure through vanity.

In contrast, we can find a story of a very different city in St. John's Apocalypse found in the last book of the Christian Bible. It speaks of a Holy city, not built by the physical hand of man driven by his ambition, but prepared by the Holiness and sacrifice made by the Christ; coming down to meet mankind so that the Holiness of God, blessed be He, can dwell within and amongst mankind without the need of a temple or tower to go to or climb, because It and all It encompasses will be the Temple.

Now if we are not careful, we may wrongfully assume that the work of our hands, along with our ambition, is an unfulfilling work of vanity; but this is not what should be concluded by the aforementioned stories. Both cities have their purpose and place, and one cannot exist without the connection and continuance of certain elements of the other. What needs to be noticed is the ill-placed ambition of man in his base self, and how the correction of his employment of that ambition needs to be realized. Our base nature and our physical elements are not the ungodliness that causes us to fail, but should be viewed as the potential foundation provided in order to prepare a realization and connection to the next level of the Temple, and should not be viewed as a stepping stone to be left behind.

A Concept of Awakening

If humanity's happiness was provided within the rudimentary connection to this material realm alone, then conforming to the demands of this corporeal world would be the key to fulfillment, which life itself disproves; therefore, we are not completely of this corporeal realm, but are 1/3 of it at the very most. Also, to be completely consumed by a desire to leave or rise above this world by grasping at spiritual enigmas to the point that we disconnect and isolate ourselves from all who are not seeking those same enigmas, will cause the pendulum to swing the opposite way concluding the same results to be the realization of a lack of fulfillment, because we are at the very most 1/3 spiritual. So, an understanding of where the divisional lines are and how to connect them is essential to our Masonic fulfillment. If you recall within the *Louisiana Masonic Monitor*, this is alluded to by the WM in his communication to every candidate in the preparation room, but usually not initially understood. So, it is clear that before growth and fulfillment can take place, one must realize the divisional lines within one's self.

The Step

The Entered Apprentice Degree is the first step within this realization, and pertains to the laws of nature, society, and Brotherhood. It is the first step away from barbarism, and into Light. It is an instructed step in the dark, and a provisional portion of Light revealing that you are not alone in your obligation and work. This is what makes the EA Degree so important and continuously relevant within the work of a Mason. This Degree pertains to a symbolic dislodging of one's original connection to the social and physical ties to the mass populace, and how one is to work within it going forward. In the Degree, a "silentude" should be experienced within the candidate's present darkness, and his unknown desire for Light is spoken of and requested for him to ensure the silence of his base desire. The Degree signifies a type of conception or birth, which begins when the candidate realizes he is separated and in darkness. The first divisional line is realized, and a separation of the elements is performed in order to alchemically change the first element, and prepare it for a future connection to the next Degree. Just as our great symbol is never permanently separated from itself or fused forever to itself, but is transformed through a gradual separation and reconnection; such is this process alluded to of our self throughout each Degree.

So, we must conclude that passing from one Degree to another does not mean that we have moved beyond the previous Degree, but have gone through it and continue to carry its work and Light with us. It is clear that the Entered Apprentice Degree is the foundation degree of Freemasonry, and should be rightfully valued as such.

A Concept of Division

One commonality with all the ancient mysteries is the basic division of man. In Manly P Hall's lecture on San Juan's (also known as St. John of the Cross) *"The Dark Night of the Soul"* it states that *"man has three natures, or parts, of which the highest and first is essentially spiritual; the second, psychic, or belonging to the sphere of soul; and the third, material, bodily or corporeal, relating to the realm of body."* It is also stated in that same text saying, *"Materialism is not man's natural way; it is a way forced upon him by exterior factors, or by the confusion in his own nature and life."* Other examples of the division can be found in books like Rabbi Joseph Gikatilla's *"Gates of Light"*, where it explains the elements of man are divided and identified as *"the Nefesh (the living force), the Ruach (the spirit), and the Neshamah (the Divine soul)."* The division of the corporeal is also evident in relation to the sun working through the Zodiac. It is noted in 32° Robert Hewitt Brown's *"Stellar Theology and Masonic Astronomy"*, that *"the Royal Arch is supported by the three Cardinal Points of the Zodiac, which consists of the Vernal and Autumnal equinoctial points at the base, and the solstice point at the summit, of which the three are emblematic of the three Pillars of the Lodge."*

These divisions are important to life as we learn and know it. There is an understanding of time and course, and any imbalances of the seasons can be devastating. Now when we allow the corporeal elements to employ our psychic and spiritual energy to render profit to the corporeal only, we are dividing ourselves in a way that is cultivating confusion; one third then usurps the other two thirds, and we then suffer a deficit within our whole self. This lesson is alluded to in the explanation of the three Great Lights and the three lesser lights; as well as the 24-inch Gauge. So, the only way to create order through the chaos of confusion is to properly identify our 3 dimensional make up. We must learn how to properly pull apart and reconnect the three by understanding how one serves the other, and also by understanding the importance of the role of each and the course by which they must work. The goal of the Entered Apprentice is to begin and prepare himself for the search of Truth.

We are not required to completely understand what is in the plans or the mind of the G.A.O.T.U. That would be like trying to understand a 9-dimensional concept with a 3-dimensional mind; besides, we are able to exercise faith by these restrictions. What is required of us is to understand our 3-dimensional existences, and to understand the relevance of each one before we can properly connect it to the other. Once this is accomplished and mastered, another dimension can be introduced to us; until then, what good would it be to have access to 9 or 10 dimensions if the 3 or 4 we now have access to confuse us?

> *"...until quietism is attained, through certain continuing discipline, no individual is in a position to know the truth. For the truth is not something that is instantly available in spite of what we are; it is something ultimately available because of what we are. The mere fact that we seek truth, that we believe in it and long for it, or that we create definitions for it – this compound process is not sufficient. The individual, to attain to the state of true internal enlightenment, must recover first from confusion." "Search for reality: Part 1- The Dark Night of the Soul- Lectures on Personal Growth"- Manly P. Hall*

So, in order to understand our world as a Master Mason, we must remember the lessons taught as an Entered Apprentice. Growth can change the dynamics of how everything in our life operates. So, the things that we've mastered in the past, now take on a new characteristic in our growth. And because we do grow, there will always be a need of discipline to accompany that growth. This reminds us that we should always be willing to dislodge ourselves from the mass populace and return to a lonely silent place, and keep the lessons of this Degree within our work and knowledge; sizing ourselves up against its moral code ensuring us that our foundation is still within its circumscribed boundaries.

"Light partakes of both life and action; it is the sphere of blending" "Melchizedic and the Mystery of Fire"- Manly P. Hall

Albert Pike's Address Before
The Grand Consistory of Louisiana
By Michael R. Poll

I believe readily that you did not want the office, but the office wanted you.
~ Charles Laffon de Ladébat to Albert Pike [1]

The passage of years can sometimes elevate a historical figure into a legend. This is not always beneficial when a study of the individual is desired. A historical figure can be examined, and their actions evaluated from a more human perspective. A legend, however, can take on near supernatural qualities and the whole of their activities are sometimes not expected to be understood or completely recounted. Such is, at times, the case with Albert Pike. It is often difficult to imagine Albert Pike as *a* player (rather than as *the* player) in American Scottish Rite events of the 1800s. The monumental mark that Pike left on the *Southern Jurisdiction* can mask the fact that his influence was not always as profound as it was in his later years. Regardless of his many accomplishments, there was a time when Illustrious Brother Pike was but an inexperienced, yet promising, Mason with a blank book before him upon which it was unknown exactly what would be written.

This address, the first ever given by Pike as the presiding officer of a Scottish Rite body, gives us a rare look at the early Albert Pike. While in his later years, Pike was viewed by many as a true Master of the Scottish Rite, this address clearly calls into notice his immaturity in the Rite, and he asks for "lenient judgment" upon his "short-comings." In his address Pike is clearly humble and seems sincerely appreciative of his election. He also notes that his election to the position of Commander in Chief was politic in nature and due to "circumstances that surround us." What could have caused a political election of the untried Albert

Pike as the presiding officer of the *Grand Consistory of Louisiana*? Let's take a look at the "circumstances."

Just seven years prior to Pike's assuming the leadership of the *Grand Consistory of Louisiana*, the whole of Louisiana Masonry underwent a dramatic shift in direction, leadership, and character. Louisiana was the most "foreign" Grand Lodge (as well as state) in the U.S. Over time, many did not view this as an acceptable situation. There was a desire to "be like everyone else." Albert Pike, however, played no part in the troubled events in Louisiana Masonry before the merger of the two Grand Lodges in Louisiana and the *Concordat of 1855*.

Albert Pike was an attorney by profession and a Mason of only five years when he moved his law practice to New Orleans in 1855.[2] Three years earlier, Pike received the Scottish Rite degrees up to the 32° from Albert Mackey in Charleston. Mackey saw a unique quality in Pike and recruited him to be on the ritual committee of the *Charleston Supreme Council*. Mackey lent Pike a collection of Scottish Rite rituals for his review and study. It was through the examination and transcription of these rituals that Pike received his first understanding of the AASR. Busy with setting up his law practice and studying the rituals lent to him by Mackey, Pike did not concern himself with the momentous developments taking place in New Orleans at the time of his arrival.

One of Pike's earliest Masonic acquaintances in New Orleans was Charles Laffon de Ladébat. Over the years (even after Pike became Grand Commander) these two would maintain a "love/hate" relationship that was founded on a basic respect for each other. Ladébat was made a 33° by James Foulhouze in the *Supreme Council of Louisiana* on February 11, 1852 and served as its Grand Secretary at the time of the *Concordat of 1855*. Ladébat would later be elected an Active Member of the *Charleston Supreme Council* in 1859. Pike's time in New Orleans put him in close contact with many competent New Orleans 33rds who were quite capable of completing Pike's education and understanding of the AASR Ladébat was, clearly, one of Pike's early mentors.

Just as he had done with Albert Mackey, Pike greatly impressed the New Orleans Scottish Rite Masons. Pike's talent and raw abilities clearly made him a candidate for any Masonic office. The fact that Pike played no part whatsoever in the *Concordat of 1855* may have made Pike even more attractive and a prime candidate for leading the *Grand Consistory of Louisiana*. Pike did not carry baggage with him from the Louisiana Masonic turmoil. While he was under the jurisdiction of the *Charleston Supreme Council* at the time of the concordat, he was not an Active Member and played no part in any of the decisions concerning the *Concordat*. No one could blame Pike for any of the events. Albert Pike was the only serious candidate for leading the *Grand Consistory* who could be seen as potentially objective as well as extraordinarily promising. Next to James Foulhouze, no one had a better chance of appeasing the French Masons and unifying all the factions. Once the *Supreme Council of Louisiana* was re-organized, Pike's value to the Charleston cause was even more evident.

This address, given by Pike only four days after he received the 33°,[3] is valuable to all Scottish Rite researchers not only because it is an extremely rare piece of early Pike literature, but also because of significant information provided in it. From this address we not only get a better feel of the early Albert Pike, but also have the opportunity to develop a more detailed understanding of the momentous events that were taking place at the time Albert Pike arrived on the Scottish Rite stage. Within just two years from the time of this address, Pike would be elected an Active Member of the *Southern Jurisdiction* (over the apparent objections of the Grand Commander and Lt. Grand Commander[4]) and then on January 2, 1859, with the very first SJ election of officers (a dramatic change in practice), be elected to the position of Sovereign Grand Commander.

Pike's address was ordered to be recorded in the handwritten Minutes of the *Grand Consistory of Louisiana*. A typed transcript of this address was made by an unknown Brother sometime between the 1940s and 1950s and a copy of this transcript acquired by this writer. The accuracy of the transcript was verified by this writer by a comparison of the transcript with the original Minutes located in the Scottish Rite Bodies of New Orleans.

Address Before the Grand Consistory of Louisiana

By Albert Pike
April 29, 1857

Th∴ Ill∴ Bros∴ and Sublime Princes of the Royal Secret:

I pray you to accept my most sincere thanks and profoundest gratitude for the great and unexpected honor which you conferred upon me, when, in my absence, you selected me to fill the most honorable and very responsible station of Grand Commander of this Grand Consistory and for your present ratification of that choice. I will earnestly endeavor to have myself not wholly undeserving of your good opinion; so that, although it must now be said that when elected I was not worthy either by service or qualification, it may not hereafter be said that when I cease to serve, you repented of your selection.

I can bring to your service, Princes, little more than good intentions, kind feelings, and a zealous devotion to the interest of Masonry of all Rites — when you find me deficient (and wherein shall I not, alas, be found, Bros∴?) I entreat of you in advance lenient judgment upon my short-comings, and that you will kindly aid me with your sympathy, support and advice. For I must be ever embarrassed by the reflection that I have been by your too favorable judgment preferred to many eminent and distinguished Brethren, whose longer service and greater familiarity with the work gave them far higher claims than any I could have preferred to the post of honor and command. If I supposed that personal consideration or a belief in my superior fitness and capacity had led you to this choice, I should sink under a sense of my feebleness, not ever have succeeded in overcoming my repugnance to accept a post where so much was to be expected. But, amass that there were other reasons, which acted upon you, and made your selection seem politic and for the interest of Masonry in this Valley, reasons not personal to me, but growing out of the conditions of things and the circumstances that surrounded us. I am encouraged to hope that I may in some degree aid in attaining the result which you all desire, and that your just expectations may not be disappointed.

I have accordingly accepted the post which you have tendered me, and will endeavor to perform its duties. Most important private business will compel my absence for some months. I shall return as soon as practicable, and remain thereafter permanently in the city.[5]

Should the interest of the Order at any time be likely to suffer by my temporary absence, I shall be prepared at once to surrender up my office, faintly imitating the lofty magnanimity, of which so beautiful an example has been set me by an Ill∴ Bro∴ whose genius and labors have done so much to restore the splendors of the Ancient and Accepted Rite[6] in this Valley, and whose name will not be forgotten among us, while the order of Knights Rose Croix continues to exist, or the Kadosh to war against tyranny and usurpation.

But I shall most sensibly feel how great will be the contrast between myself, with my slender experience, and the Th∴ Ill∴ Prince and Sovereign whose place I come to take, but not fill.[7] Eminent in Masonic learning and more illustrious by long and faithful service than even by his high rank and lofty station, the new and supreme dignity recently conferred upon him was a most just and appropriate acknowledgment of his worth. This Consistory must most sensibly feel its loss, as he, Ill∴ Gr ∴ Commander, crowned and laureled with the highest honor, and with the grateful thanks and recollections of his brethren, most gracefully retires from this distinguished post, to yield it of his own choice to another. I beseech him not to withdraw from me his counsel and advice, and I pray him and our Ill∴ Bro∴ Laffon,[8] and the other eminent brethren who surround me, to aid me, to advise me, to support me in my inexperience, that, guided by them I may not despair of rendering some little service to the cause of humanity, to the cause of truth, of liberty, of philosophy, and of Masonic progress.

My brethren, I see around me the representatives of more than one race,[9] and the disciples of more than one Masonic Rite — I rejoice at this reunion, and it gives me happy augury of the prosperity, health, and continuance of Masonry in this Valley. I am especially glad that here and in other bodies of this Rite, I see by the side of the children of the first generous and gallant settlers of Louisiana, many of another land, and who not long since for the first time passed beyond the boundaries of the York Rite.

We are all aware, my brethren, how little among Masons of the latter Rite is known of the Ancient & Accepted Rite, and how great and general a prejudice has obtained those against it. It has been imagined that there was antagonism between the two: Scottish Masonry has been deemed almost spurious, and its degrees, at the best, no more than mere side degrees; and the York Mason who has entered into our sanctuaries has been regarded in the estimation of many, as untrue to his allegiance and disloyal.

Those of you, my brethren, who lately have known only the York Rite, are already aware how unfounded is this prejudice, how erroneous this opinion, how chimerical these apprehensions and alarms. It shall be my study to make you more fully to know this hereafter.

The Ancient and Accepted Rite is, when itself fully developed and understood, when itself what it should be and can be, a great, harmonious and connected system, all the degrees and lessons, embody the philosophy, the history, the morality and the essential meaning of Masonry, and are to us what the Ancient mysteries were to the initiate of Eleusis, of Egypt, and of Samothrace.

The degrees of this Rite are commentaries on the Master's Degree, which itself is essentially the same in all Rites. They interpret instead of being at variance with that degree. They ultimately make it known to the Initiate the true word and the true meaning and inner sense of the True Word of a Mason. They teach the great doctrines that God taught the Patriarchs, and which are the foundations on which all religions repose.

We do not undervalue symbolic Masonry, nor love it the less because we also love the Ancient & Accepted Rite, we but learn justly to value the Master's degree, by coming to understand its full meaning and to appreciate the sublime and lofty lessons which it teaches. Masonry is one everywhere and in all its Temples of whatever Rite; as it has been one in all times. Everywhere it teaches the same great lessons of morality and philosophy, or should do so, if faithful to its mission, and if its apostles are properly informed and true to the duties which it imposes on them. If anywhere it has excluded from even the inmost Sanctuaries of its Temples men of any faith who believe in Our Supreme God, Creator and Preserver of all things that become, and in the immortality of the Soul-if it has anywhere assumed the garb of religious exclusion and intolerance, of Jesuitism, of political vengeance, of Hermetic Mysticism, there most assuredly it has ceased to be Masonry.

It would not be true to say, however, that even Scottish Masonry has adequately fulfilled or been equal to its missions. While by the irresistible influence of time, by innovations and by mutilations and corruptions of ignorance, the degrees of the York Rite have long since ceased to be what they should be, and what they were in the beginning, when they succeeded to those ancient academies of science, philosophy and morality, the mysteries; while the practice of confirming everything contained in them to the memory has by the silent lapse of time caused more and more both of ceremony and substance to be forgotten, much to be intentionally dropped, and the field of each degree to be made more and more narrow; while the true meaning of very many of their most valuable symbols have faded away and disappeared, and been replaced by commonplace, and the inventions of ignorance, and the lofty science and profound teachings, of the Ancients have too much given way to unimpressive phrases and valueless formulas, — the Scottish Rite also has not enjoyed immunity from the ravages of the biting tooth of time, universal destroyer of all human beings.

For even here, where over the Temples of our Degrees stood perfect and complete in all the splendor and Majesty of their beautiful and harmonious proportions, we are like strangers from a far land who wander amid the shattered columns and wrecked glories of Thebes and Palmyra, and union over the ruins that track the steps of time, and over the instability of all earthly things. From many of our degrees everything has dropped out except the signs and words, and they remain half effaced and corrupted. From more, all is lost except these and some unimportant formulas; in still more, useless repetition arrives at impressiveness, but cannot renunciate us for the old science and the noble philosophy whose place it endeavors to supply. Those huge chasms have been created in the work, and the connections between the degrees have been broken; so that each has become a fragment instead of being, as at first part of one consistent, regularly progressive and harmonious whole.

Thus it has come that of the degrees from the fourth to the thirty-second inclusive, which we retain and apply to ourselves the sounding titles, four only are habitually conferred, which all the residue remain in a great measure, and part of them altogether unknown.

It had become so obvious that this Rite needed reformation, and that either its degrees should all be made worthy to be conferred and of value to be attained, or else those which were not so ought to be abandoned and their titles disused, that more than two years ago the Supreme

Council at Charleston appointed a Committee of five Brethren to revise the whole ritual of the degrees; on which Committee I had the distinguished honor to be placed. While my Brother Laffon, both before and after he was also placed there in the stead of my Brother Samory, who to the general regret found himself compelled to decline the act.[10] While my Brother Laffon labored, more particularly on the 18th Degree, but not alone on that, I also, undertaking at first a few degrees, continued my labors during two years, until I completed a revision of all; which that it may be thoroughly examined and sanctioned, I have printed in a volume and submitted to the Supreme Council. Whether that August Body will stamp it or any part of it with its approval, is wholly unknown to me. I have endeavored to restore the effaced or faded lineament of many of the degrees to develop and elaborate the great leading idea of each, to correct the whole together as a regular series, and to make of them our harmonious and systematic whole, ascending by regular graduations to the highest moral and philosophical truth — I have endeavored to prime away all commonplaces and puerility's, all unmeaning forms and ceremonies, all absurd interpretations, and everything useless or injurious with which time and ignorance had overloaded the degrees. I have endeavored so to restore, to retouch and to supply, retaining all that was valuable and working up all the old material, as to make every degree worth to be conferred: that there should be no longer any empty tile, or barren honors in the Ancient & Accepted Rite.

This I have attempted; but I am only too well aware that the undertaking was too great for my furios; and that what I have done will be found full of imperfections, as the work of the painter, the sculpture, the creator, and the poet ever falls short of his own ideal.

Still I have endeavored to do somewhat; and it is my desire, at some appropriate future time, and with your consent and assistance, to confer upon some suitable candidate such of the degrees, as I have revised them, as have not been already revised by other and more competent hands.

I congratulate you, my brethren, on the advancement and progress of the Ancient & Accepted Rite in this Valley: The Concordat by which the Supreme Jurisdiction of the Supreme Council at Charleston was acknowledged and under which the two Consistories then existing became one, laid broad and deep the strong foundations of the prosperity of our Rite. The walls of our Temple solidly and squarely built, bid defiance to the storms of faction; and if we are true to ourselves, peace will dwell within our gates.

And in the Realm of Masonry, if anywhere on earth, there ought to be peace and quiet and harmony. Nowhere are schism and faction, and disunion and discontent so lamentably out of place as here. Here there should be no lust for power and no eagerness for rank or distinction. If discontented men should in this valley have established, or if any shall hereafter establish, under a foreign authority which has no jurisdiction here and act only by usurpation, any body or bodies, claiming to administer the Ancient & Accepted Rite, we shall, I think, be prepared to show that the Supreme Council at Charleston, to which we owe allegiance, is the only legitimate authority in the Rite that can exist in our country south of the River Potomac; and that the Grand Orient of France and the Supreme Council within its bosom offered against Masonic Law and Masonic Comity where they made another jurisdiction and erect their banners on the soil of Louisiana.

It is time that this question should be receive the fullest consideration; and that the authentic history of the creation of the Grand Orient itself and of that of the Supreme Council of France, of the disputes between those two bodies and their temporary alliance should be made known to the order in the United States. Supplied with the emissary documents on both sides, it is every intention to translate them and make them public, that all may judge where is the right and where the usurpation.

The time when fables would pass for history has gone by; and that has come when criticism and investigation will deal with the history of Masonry as with other histories, separating the truth from the error, and after reducing great pretensions to the narrowest proportions. Let us examine the history the Ancient & Accepted Rite and the Grand Orient in that spirit and by the rules and canons of sound criticism, never forgetting that courtesy, moderation, and kindness ought to inspire all Masonic discussions, hoping to find a like tone and spirit on the other side, and that those who may array themselves against us will, if Right and Truth be found with us, candidly admit it, and uniting with us acknowledge the same allegiance and so cause peace ever and ever to reign in this valley.

My Brethren let me impress it upon you, that there is much to do, if we would have Masonry adequately fulfill its mission. It is not sufficient merely to receive three or four of the degrees, and then, imagining the rest, to live in contented indolence, without an effort to know the high science and philosophy of the system. The time has come when one who would be truly and really be a Scottish Rite Mason must study and reflect. It shall be my earnest endeavor to aid you in penetrating to the inmost heart of Masonry and in unveiling its profound secrets, which are that light towards which all Masons at least profess to struggle, that knowledge of the True Work which is the great remuneration of a Mason's labor. But if I should fall short of the performance of this duty, be not you, my brethren, disheartened nor discouraged. Masonry must be true to itself, or it will find in numbers weakness only, and its walls will be crushed to the ground with its own might. In this intellectual and practical age. Masonry must it from merited disaster and dissolution.

It is time for it to assume a higher ground; and here, if anywhere, the effort to elevate it must be made. Here, I believe, we can commence and successfully carry onward the indispensable work of reformation, that shall in time end the reign of puerility's and trivialities, and make masonry what it should be. The great teacher of moral and philosophical truth; the teacher of the primitive religion known to the first men that lived; the defender of the right of free thought, free conscience and free speech; the apostle of rational and well-regulated liberty; the protector of the oppressed, the defender of the common people, the asserter of the dignity of labor and the right of the laboring man; the enemy of intolerance, fanaticism and uncharitable opinion, and of all idle and pernicious theories that arraign providence for its dispensations, and endeavor to set their notions of an abstract justice and equality above the laws by which God chooses to rule all human affairs.

In this great work I wish your co-operation, and I ask, for myself and for those eminent brethren who are to act with me and in my place, your countenance, your assistance, and your encouragement. I am sure my brethren that I shall not ask this in vain; and that grateful, deeply grateful as I now am for your confidence and kindness, I shall be far more so, and with far greater reason, when I am allowed to surrender into your hands the trust which you have so generously confided to me.

Notes:

1. Charles Laffon de Ladébat to Albert Pike, June 24, 1860. Archives of the *Supreme Council, 33°, SJ*, Washington. Photocopy in possession of the author.
2. Pike's law office was located in downtown New Orleans in a building on the riverside of Camp Street one block from Canal Street. The building no longer exists. *New Orleans City Directory*, 1856.
3. After the *Concordat of 1855*, the Active Members of the *New Orleans Supreme Council* were brought in as Honorary Members of the *Charleston Supreme Council*. As with all Honorary Members of a Supreme Council, they held the 33° but not the active office of Sovereign Grand Inspector General (SGIG). It was at this time that the *Charleston Supreme Council* began elevating 32° Masons to the 33° but not including the office of SGIG in their elevation. Albert

Pike was one of the first 32° in the SJ elevated to the 33° without being invested with the office of SGIG Pike would be elected an Active Member (SGIG) of the *Charleston Supreme Council* on March 20,1858.

4. "*. ..I was not the last to devise the means of placing you at the head of the order, 1st by making you a 33rd against the will of Messrs. Furman & Honour: 2nd by vacating my office of Deputy in your favor, & twice you got in the S.C. & especially twice you were unanimously elected to the Presidency, I consider myself as having done my duty, all I could do. The lifeless council of Charleston was revived; it lives now! Only now tho!*" Ladébat to Pike, Jun. 24, 1860.

5. *The New Orleans City Directories* from 1856 until 1859 show that while Pike had opened a law office in New Orleans, he did not have more than a temporary home in the city. The Minutes of the *Grand Consistory* also reveal that he was absent for many of the meetings of the *Grand Consistory*. There is no record that Pike ever moved his family to New Orleans, and it is probable that he traveled between his home in Little Rock and New Orleans. One of the many boarding houses in New Orleans would have likely been his residence during his stays in the city. Despite Pike's statement, New Orleans would never be his permanent home.

6. At the time of this address, the term *Ancient and Accepted Scottish Rite* was not in common use in the U.S. This accounts for Pike's repeated use of the older (in the U.S.) term *Ancient and Accepted Rite*.

7. Pike refers to Claude Pierre Samory. Samory was elected an Active Member of the *Charleston Supreme Council* on Nov. 20, 1856.

8. Charles Laffon de Ladébat.

9. Freemasonry in pre-Civil War New Orleans was reflective of the New Orleans culture of the time. Pierre Roup was the son-in-law of New Orleans Mason and Battle of New Orleans hero Dominique Youx. Roup was a member of *Perseverance Lodge No. 4* and sat on the lodge's building committee. He was an African-American Creole. While it is clear that there were more than a few African-American Creoles who were members of New Orleans lodges, identifying them is difficult as a member's race was not a question asked or recorded except in notable situations. It is quite possible that there were African-American Creole members of the *Grand Consistory of Louisiana* present at the time of Pike's address. It is, likewise, possible that Pike used the word "race" in reference to the French Masons who were often considered part of the "Latin race".

10. On p. 249 of his *History of the Supreme Council 33°, A.&A.S.R. S.J., U.S.A (1801- 1864)* (Washington: Supreme Council, 33°, 1964) Ray Baker Harris, 33°, reproduces a letter sent by Albert Mackey to Claude Samory dated Mar. 21, 1855. The letter concerns the *Southern Jurisdiction's* Ritual Committee and lists its members. Claude Samory is listed as the member from New Orleans and Albert Pike the member from Little Rock. Ill. Harris writes: "*From all indications, the 'preparation of new copies' was in the hands of Albert Pike. He was then in New Orleans, and may have conferred with Samory in this work, but neither of them ever mentioned such a collaboration in their numerous letters written in this period.*" Until this address by Pike was rediscovered, it was assumed by most Scottish Rite scholars that Samory was on this committee with Pike for a substantial period of time. Bro. Harris, assuming that Samory remained on the committee, logically wondered about the absence of communications between Pike and Samory concerning ritual matters. This address brings to light the fact that Samory retired from the committee shortly after his appointment to be replaced by Ladébat. The collaboration was not between Pike and Samory, but between Pike and Ladébat and renders the degrees written by the two and their communications understandable.

Cornerstone Principles of The Masonic Philosophy
By Clayton J. "Chip" Borne, III, PGM

As a young child, I lived in a perfect world or so I thought. Insecurity was not part of my wonderful existence. My parents, grandparents, aunts and uncles and even great aunts and uncles always had time and always made me feel special, secure and loved. One Saturday morning my Father came to me with a pensive look on his normally smiling face. I asked "Dad, why are you sad?" He sat me down and said that one of my favorite great aunts had passed away. In a heartbeat, my perception of life changed. My perfect world with all its special people would never be the same again. All of those that I loved, especially my parents would one day like my favorite aunt, be gone. For the first time, I felt insecurity and fear.

Knowing that the reality of death had affected me, my Dad sat me down and told me that it was part of God's infinite plan, which design included the assurance that there was another life where we would all be together again for eternity. It was the story of a Supreme Being, "God" who had as part of his creation an elegant plan for eternal life which for us as Christians embraced the Holy Trinity. That assurance created an immediate sense of security quieting my newfound fear. The experience, as I would later learn as an adult, was the Cornerstone Principle of the Masonic Philosophy. Its defining principles are revealed to each Brother as an educational reward in his search for light. They are as follows:

It has been written that "Life is not merely a series of meaningless accidents, chance encounters or coincidences, but rather, it is a complexity of events that culminate in an exquisite subline order." This philosophical principle mandates an acceptance of a Creator, a First Cause, a Supreme Being, or as described in Freemasonry, the Grand Architect of the Universe. The conviction has been and continues to be the essential predicate to the masonic philosophy. The philosophy also creates an empirical desire to understand creation and the development of life.

Freemasonry is the Oldest and Most Dynamic Fraternal Brotherhood the World has ever known having as its Primary Objective to unite good men in a common bond for a better world. Its essence is found in the spiritual support of the most basic or fundamental causes in the development and defense of Humanity namely Charity, Opposition to Materialism and a Defense of Human Dignity. It is a philosophical institution embracing the preservation of social, political and religious liberty and all subjects pertaining to the welfare of man as an intellectual and social creature.

Freemasonry is a Universal Brotherhood of men whose discipline turns to God for praise and prayer. Its Heart is given to those men who of their own free will and accord desire its principles. The Order employs tools of ethical and moral truth to serve mankind. It travels the road of peace and harmony, guided by the principles of Fidelity, Unselfishness and Kindness. Those active disciplines pursued by the Brotherhood create the means by which and through which our Creator, God, the Grand Architect of the Universe, bestows his blessings on mankind.

Freemasonry is an Initiate Order with its discipline fostering the development, enhancement and transformation of the individual through a lifelong process of Self-Improvement. As the ancient operatives used their skills to build lasting monuments of stone, speculative masons strive to build character emphasizing the internal rather than the external qualifications of man. The order holds in veneration loyalty to God, Family and Country.

Freemasonry's Obedience's embrace Knowledge, Wisdom and Honor. Its Royal status is given to men who sincerely desire its principles in their hearts. Freemasonry is a Way of Life created by a desire for immortality its disciplines lead men from darkness into a never-ending search for light. The Enlightened Brotherhood answers the Cries of Humanity, the Sick, the Poor, and the Distressed.

Freemasonry embraces the Basic Virtues of Brotherly Love, Relief and Truth. It is dedicated to the Cardinal Virtues of Fortitude, Prudence, Temperance and Justice which ideals encourage each member to preserve an upright character and a maturing civility in all his dealings with his fellow man.

Freemasonry's Historical Research becomes an addicting phenomenon which captures our realities as well as our fantasies. Its reflections are found embedded in the Ancient Mysteries, with its moral code assuming responsibility for Justice, Truth, Freedom, Liberty, Honesty, and Integrity in all respects of Human Endeavor. Its pursuit awakens the Tribal emotion within each of us to learn more of the Brothers who have completed their labors in this reality and the disciplined philosophy by which they lived their lives.

After an extensive study of the History of our Order, I submit as a premise for this Thesis that Freemasonry's identity can be found collectively interwoven with the Social, Spiritual and Economic Development of Humanity. The Order binds like-minded men into a Brotherhood that transcends all religious, social, cultural, ethnic and educational differences. Freemasonry and its moral code in this Author's opinion constitute a Philosophy of Life which by definition has existed since time immemorial among men of good will. Its mysteries are revealed in the Natural Law of Creation common in diverse societies that embrace the three symbolic ideals of Wisdom, Strength and Beauty. Freemasonry's footprints to the enlightened eye can be seen permanently imprinted on the diachronic pages of time. Its discipline will travel into eternity and will continue to be Freemasonry.

Bibliography

Hall, Manly: *Secret Teachings of All Ages*, 1928 Philosophical Research Society

Pike, Albert: *The Meaning of Freemasonry*, 1924, Masonic Service Assn. Pg. 32, 33, 36, 37

Hutchins: *Pillars of Wisdom*, Revised 1995, Pg. 9

Foulhouze, James: *Historical Inquiries into the Origin of Freemasonry*, SR 1859

McCosh, Joseph: *Documents Upon Sublime Freemasonry*, Oct. 10, 1802, Pg. 17

Bogdam and Shoek: *Handbook of Freemasonry*, Prescott Editors, Ch 2 & 3, 2014

Pike, Albert: *Grand Constitutions of Freemasonry, Ancient & Accepted Rite*, Pg. 1, 184 280, 299

Meaningful Myths, Truer than Facts.

By Taylor Nauta

There is a broken pillar in the world of religion today, especially in the Christian religion as we know it in the West. Perhaps this pillar was first cracked by the Great Schism of 1054, further damaged by the Protestant Reformation, and then finally broken by the Enlightenment, which caused an unnecessary tug-o-war between science and faith; as if the two are somehow at odds with each other. Years of scandals have led many people to question the authority of the Magisterium, and then certain scientific discoveries have led even more to question the literal truthfulness of the Bible. After all this commotion over the past millennia, some people have discarded their faith in God altogether while others have rigidly held on to blind faith in spite of all evidence that contradicts their world view. St Thomas Aquinas once said, "The truth of our faith becomes a matter of ridicule among the infidels if any Catholic, not gifted with the necessary scientific learning, presents as dogma what scientific scrutiny shows to be false." How right he was! That's precisely what has continued to happen after the Enlightenment; and there now stands a rift between two sides who both interpret the Bible too literally. One side refuses to believe in the Bible stories on account of the fact that certain parts just don't stand up to scientific scrutiny, and the other side believes in the total historicity of the Bible stories in spite of that fact. One side embraces science and modernity, and the other embraces tradition; accepting what they've always been taught, presupposing it to be factually true, never questioning their worldview for fear of losing their eternal rewards. Both sides of this false dichotomy are in error, of course. One side is guilty of throwing the baby out with the bath water, and the other side is guilty of confirmation bias. One side is too skeptical, and the other side is too superstitious. Indeed, there is a broken pillar in the world of religion today. The middle pillar. The harmonic center between two extremes. The broken pillar in religion today is mysticism; a contemplative lifestyle; an interior way of understanding the exterior language of religious myth.

The way I see it, atheists and fundamentalists have one thing in common: they both fail to see the symbolic significance of myth. They both conflate truth with fact. They both think that something is untrue unless it is factually or literally true. This is folly. A myth is not merely fiction. A myth is often true in the truest sense of truthfulness. The archetypal, timeless, forever sense of Truth. Whereas a factual narrative contains truth about something that happened once upon a time in history at some specific geographic locale, a mythical narrative contains truth about something that is happening here, now, and always. Factual narratives are true in the sense that they are accounts of events that happened once, whereas mythical narratives are true in the sense that they are about events which are always happening.... within us all. The world needs to realize that the sacred scriptures are not mere history lessons. Rather, they are reality lessons. Many of the stories in the Bible are allegorical, symbolic, metaphorical, mythical narratives written in historical contexts relative to the their respective audiences; and though the historical aspects of these stories are important, these stories are primarily intended to teach you lessons about reality that straightforward language lacks the potency to convey. Their primary function is not necessarily to give you a history lesson, but rather to give you a lesson pertaining to the ineffable, Ultimate Reality that is God at the center and circumference of all existence. Religious myths are archetypal allegories designed to deliver insight into the mysterious nature of God, the human condition, and the Divine-human relationship.

Albert Pike once said, "The symbols of the wise always become the idols of the ignorant multitude." (Morals & Dogma, pp. 818-819) Truer words have never been spoken. Imagine a teacher pointing his finger at the moon, but his students are so focused on his finger that they fail to see what he was pointing at; and so, they overlook the moon entirely. That's how it is with most people when they read the Bible, or any other works written by ancient mystics. They get too hung up on the details, too entrenched in a literalistic interpretation, and they mistake the symbol for that which it was intended to symbolize.

The wise philosophers of all ages have used allegory and symbolism as their main modes of teaching, for how else do you help people understand something that transcends all finite concepts? How else do you discuss the ineffable? How else do you describe that which is utterly beyond words? Metaphor is the best way, of course. It is the only way. You have to make the ineffable effable by putting it in a story that is deeply true in essence, completely true in a figurative sense, though it may not necessarily be true in a literal sense. This is why Jesus spoke in parables. For example, think of these verses from the gospel of Matthew where Jesus used parables to describe the Kingdom of Heaven by way of analogy.

He said, *"The kingdom of heaven is like unto a grain of mustard seed, which a man took, and sowed in his field: which indeed is the least of all seeds: but when it is grown, it is the greatest among herbs, and becometh a tree, so that the birds of the air come and lodge in the branches thereof."* (Matthew 13:31-32) *"....the kingdom of heaven is like unto treasure hid in a field; the which when a man hath found, he hideth, and for joy thereof goeth and selleth all that he hath, and buyeth that field."* (Matthew 13:44) *"...the kingdom of heaven is like unto a merchant man, seeking goodly pearls: Who, when he had found one pearl of great price, went and sold all that he had, and bought it."* (Matthew 13:45) *"...the kingdom of heaven is like unto a net, that was cast into the sea, and gathered of every kind: Which, when it was full, they drew to shore, and sat down, and gathered the good into vessels, but cast the bad away."* (Matthew 13:47-48)

2020 Transactions of the Louisiana Lodge of Research

The Bible is full of symbolic language, with metaphorical poetry being intermingled with prose from Genesis to the Revelation of Saint John and everywhere in between. This is because the subject matter at which it aims - i.e., God - is beyond words. Ineffable. Poetry describes Him better than prose, for poetry is symbolic in nature; but alas, even poetry must inevitably fall short. Language has limitations, but God is limitless.

St Augustine of Hippo is a good example of an early Christian theologian who intuitively knew that words and concepts will always fall short of accurately describing God.

He said, *"If you understood him, it would not be God." "God is more truly imagined than expressed, and He exists more truly than He is imagined." "God is not what you imagine or what you think you understand. If you understand, you have failed."*

Taken literally, many stories in the Bible and other sacred books are full of absurdities; and one must virtually ignore his reasoning and critical thinking faculties in order to believe them as facts. Especially when believing them to be factually true requires ignoring all scientific evidence to the contrary. But when understood figuratively, the stories of the Bible, the Vedas, the Upanishads, and other holy books are pregnant with meaning. Indeed, there are incredibly profound depths of truth in them.

True faith is not merely a matter of naively believing stories or statements about God to be factually true; but rather trusting in the reality that is God at the center and circumference of all existence. One might say that God is being itself, the very wellspring of is-ness, in whom we live, move, and have our being. Being eternal, He obviously predates any name that has ever been ascribed to Him. "I Am that I Am" was the name by which He introduced Himself to Moses, after all.

"And God said unto Moses, I Am That I Am: and he said, Thus shall thou say unto the children of Israel, I Am hath sent me

unto you." (Exodus 3:14)

He is who He is, self-existent and eternal; infinitely beyond the finite comprehension of the human intellect. He's not some old man in the sky who disapprovingly wags his finger at us all when we think naughty thoughts or eat foods prohibited by the Kosher laws as written in Leviticus. He's omnipresent, and thus there can be no place where He is absent. Every atom in the universe is completely saturated and surrounded by Him. We cannot escape God any more than light can escape a flame. This being so, God's abode, the Kingdom of Heaven, isn't some distant locale, but rather a plane of consciousness that exists within us all. It's the eternal now, whether we're present enough to be aware of it or not. It's the metaphysical reality that underlies our physical reality as we know it. This metaphysical reality is more real than physical reality. Whereas physical reality, or the world of the senses, is one of constant change and motion, the metaphysical reality of God is one of constant, unchanging, eternal stillness. In comparison to this eternal reality that is the Kingdom God, the transient reality of life as we know it is but a dream. A symbolic myth pointing to something greater. Something within.

"Neither shall they say, Lo here! or, lo there! for, behold, the kingdom of God is within you." (Luke 17:21)

It's cognitive dissonance to hold two conflicting beliefs at the same time. Thus, it's silly to believe that we can ever be separated from the presence of an omnipresent God. We're never separated from Him! How could we be? He is the ultimate reality in whom "we live, move, and have our being," as St Paul so eloquently said in Acts 17:28. He's always present. He's above, below, within and without; and this is true whether we are aware of it or not. The only thing that can come between us and our God is our own pride. Pride is the forbidden fruit that results in us being exiled from the Garden of Eden - i.e., the awareness of God's presence - because we become so preoccupied with our ego that we forget about our true Self and its First Estate. When we get caught up in egocentrism and the illusion of materialism, we become blind to the true nature of reality. We fail to realize that God is within us and all around us. Whenever we believe that anything can truly be placed between us and God, we are mistaken. The Roman Catholic Church made a mistake when they put a man, whom they claim to be infallible, between us and God; and the Protestants made an equally lamentable mistake when they put a book, which they claim to be infallible, between us and God. No-one is infallible, and no-thing is infallible. No-one and no-thing but God Himself, of course. He being nearer to us than our own breath, no man or book written by men can stand between us and Him.

Most of us have been doing religion all wrong for a long time. We let books and traditions inform us about what God is like, which results in a secondhand kind of faith. Those who wrote the books and started the traditions had first-hand experiences with God, gaining insights which they then tried to share with the rest of humanity by way of symbolic rites and stories. It's far better to experience God yourself by turning inward, becoming aware of His presence by engaging in disciplined contemplative practices, such as centering prayer and discursive meditation, then it is to take someone else's word for it. When you've experienced the presence and reality of God yourself, your religious books and traditions then become symbolic tools and lenses to help you make sense of that ineffable experience. The sacramental stories and rituals of your religious tradition then become symbolic forms that illustrate infinite truths in ways that make sense to our finite understanding, which is limited to the perception of just five senses. It becomes clear that God didn't write those stories, nor did He establish any rites. Humans wrote those stories and established rites in response to their experiences with God; the Sacred; the Infinite; the Ineffable. Thus, the Bible is not a divine product written by God. Rather, it is a human product, written by humans in response to their experience with God. As such, it is certainly inspired; but it is obviously not infallible. There is an incredible amount of truth in it, however. Truth pertaining to the human condition, the mysterious nature of reality, and the Divine-human relationship.

So, then, what is Christianity really about if the Bible stories aren't merely to be taken literally? Love. It's about a life centered in Love, which God is, and it's about seeking first the Kingdom of Heaven wherein Love is the law. Love for God and our fellow man. It's about a Way of transformation. It's about being a disciple, a follower of the example set by Jesus; for he was love incarnate. He was and is God's character and passion embodied in a human person.

Jesus Christ is indeed the Way, the Truth and the Life; even if his story is entirely mythical (although I don't believe it is). Whether or not he was literally conceived via immaculate conception, born of a virgin, crucified to atone for the sins of the world, and resurrected on the third day, to me he is still nevertheless the ultimate personification of God's love for mankind. He is still the ultimate disclosure of what God is like, incarnate in a human form. The finite mind of man can't comprehend the infinite nature of God, but we can perhaps comprehend the unconditional love He has for us; and that love is powerfully portrayed in the life of Jesus. God is Love, and Jesus is love personified. The Word, or law, of God is Love; and Christ is that Word made flesh.

When I say I'm a Christian, I don't necessarily mean that I unquestioningly believe a bunch of statements about Jesus to be factually true. What I primarily mean is that I'm a disciple; a follower of the Way of life that Jesus embodied. But at the same time, I also believe that Jesus' story actually happened as described in the gospels. I believe that it is literally true in addition to being symbolically true. Why must it be "either or" when it could well be "both and"? I believe that life itself, with nature and all of its varied laws and actions, is allegorical. The whole of God's creation is a metaphor pointing to Him. Everything that happens in the cosmos, at all levels, from the galactic to the molecular, is symbolic and meaningful. There's purpose in all of it, and it's all incredible. Therefore, I have no doubt that God, who wills the incomprehensibly vast cosmos into being, is capable of becoming incarnate and effecting a bodily resurrection from the dead. God could definitely do that. He could do everything that the gospels of Matt, Mark, Luke and John say He did, and He very well may have. I believe He did. But even if He didn't, even if it's just a symbolic story, it is still a true story, nevertheless. It's true in the truest sense of truthfulness. Christ is not merely another hero archetype. He is the ultimate hero archetype to whom all others point. The great novelist J. R. R. Tolkien also knew this, and he gently led C. S. Lewis to the same realization one day during an interesting debate on the significance of religious myth. That conversation turned out to be a catalyst that ultimately resulted in the once atheist Lewis converting to Christianity and becoming one of the greatest Christian apologists who ever lived! Talk about a transformative dialogue!

We need to be having transformative dialogues within ourselves. That's what the scriptures are really about, if you ask me. The scriptures speak to our hearts, pointing us toward the discovery of who and what we really are in relation to God. Religion needs to return to its heart, you see; and that heart is mysticism. We need to unite the outer forms of religion with an inner understanding. We need to stop getting so hung up on literal interpretations of the Bible stories that we fail to see the treasure in them which is hidden in plain sight. We need to dig below the surface, exploring deeper layers of meaning, so that we can perceive what these stories are really about at their innermost levels. Whether or not the Bible stories actually happened once upon a time isn't as important as realizing that they symbolize dramas which are being played out within us all the time. There is a Moses within us all, just like there is a Pharaoh within us all. There is a Jesus within us all, and there is likewise a Judas within us all. The truth contained in the Bible is timeless and eternally relevant in the here and now; but we have to return to mysticism and contemplative practice to realize this. The Eastern (Orthodox) Church has done a far better job at this than the Western (Roman Catholic) Church over the past few hundred years, although the Catholic Church does have some monastic Orders that excel at it. But meditation and contemplative practice is almost nowhere to be found in the Protestant traditions, unfortunately. How sad, for it is a vitally important aspect of Christianity that has been neglected by far too many for far too long!

Christianity is about more than believing certain dogmatic doctrines to be true, it's more than paying tithing, and it's more than going to church on Sunday. Above all, Christianity ought to be a contemplative lifestyle rooted in a personal relationship with Christ. A first-hand, personal, experiential relationship with God as He is made known to us in Christ through the Holy Spirit. This sort of experiential relationship makes our traditions and holy books come to life in truly meaningful ways. Faith needs to be a way of the heart rather than just a way of the head. It's not merely about a trivial acceptance of doctrinal statements that are hard to believe when understood literally. Faith isn't necessarily about believing in the factuality of unbelievable statements so much as it's about trusting in the truthfulness of the spirit or essence which underlies those statements. It's about trusting in the reality that is God at the center and circumference of all existence. It's about trusting in the relationship that the Creator has with his creation. A relationship of love and grace, which is illustrated beautifully in the gospel. If it's illustrated better anywhere else, I know not where.

The gospel isn't merely about how to go to heaven after you die. It's also about living in the Kingdom of Heaven here and now. It's about the realization that Jesus, who is the personification of God, is Lord; and Caesar is not. God is the Supreme Ruler, and the oppressive rulers of this world are not. God is Love, and the Kingdom of Heaven is a world wherein love is the law. That's the good news! The

Kingdom of Heaven is within you! The Kingdom of Heaven is at hand! All you have to do is look within; and then you'll not only find God at the center of your own being, but you'll also find Him in your fellow man and everywhere in nature. When you emerge from the dark night of the soul that is the illusion of separation from God, you see the world from a new perspective. A non-dualistic perspective. Death to the old way of seeing and rebirth into this new way, this true way of seeing, illuminated by the Holy Spirit, is what it means to be born again. When the selfish ego within you dies on the cross of introspection, the self-emptying Savior in you is resurrected. The false self must die so that the true Self can be reborn.

You see this primordial truth illustrated in several mythical stories, and they tend to be stories that people naturally love. We love those kinds of stories because they resonate with us at the soul level. Those stories speak to the deepest desires and aspirations of the human heart, and we subconsciously know them to be figuratively true even though we consciously know them to be fictional. In so many stories, you have a hero character who descends into a secret place wherein he discovers a boon which enables him to achieve a great task of some sort. In the story of Aladdin, for example, Aladdin descends into the Cave of Wonders wherein he discovers a magic lamp containing a genie who eventually teaches him to be himself. He had previously been living his life from the outside in rather than from the inside out. He had allowed his society and culture to wrongly estimate his worth and inform him of what he ought to be like. He thought he needed wealth and titles to get the girl, but he really only needed to discover his true worth; his inner worth. In doing so, he not only got the girl, but he also defeated the villain and saved his people from tyranny. It is a story of transformation! Death and rebirth! Death to his self-centered, materialistic, old way of being, which was that of a street thief, and a rebirth into a new way of being; that of a prince due to the purity of his heart and the nobility of his character! He went into the cave seeking a treasure, and he came out of it with a treasure that he already possessed all along: his own divine potential. His true Self. He was never just a street rat. He was always more than that, but he never knew it until he looked within. So, it is with all of us. We all have to descend into the Cave of Wonders, which is at the center of our very being, to discover who and what we really are. The Self is there to be found in the darkest, innermost, hidden recess of the subconscious mind. It is preserved within a secret vault beneath the Sanctum Sanctorum of the Temple of the psyche.

You also see this same truth illustrated in the Lion King. The long-exiled Simba encounters Rifiki, a sort of shamanic character, a hierophant, a psychopomp who initiates him into mature adulthood by leading him into a secret cavern beneath a large tree. In the depths of this cavern, Simba sees his own reflection in a pool of water; and he sees a startling resemblance to his father in this reflection. He sees his potential, what he could and should be. After this, he sees a vision or apparition of his Father, Mufasa, appearing to him in the sky as a sort of solar figure. "Remember who you are", Mufasa said. Simba had forgotten that he was the son of a King. We all forget that fact, and we must turn inward to rediscover it so that we can fulfill our potential and regain control of our estate. This is what happens in the Lion King! Simba wastes his adolescence in leisure with his friends, Timon and Pumbaa, who seduce him into a carefree lifestyle with no responsibilities. But when Rafiki leads him to that hidden pool, he encounters his true Self and emerges from the experience transformed! Simba emerged from that experience reborn into a new sense of duty and purpose, going from the attitude of a selfish child to that of a selfless adult who labors for the good of others. He went from being someone who could hardly take care of himself to being one who could take care of many. He died to an old way of being and was born again into a new way of being. He woke up as if he had been asleep for a long time. Suddenly realizing that he had let his kingdom fall into disarray, he knew that he had to do something about it. He knew he had to confront Scar (the evil uncle who had tyrannically usurped his kingdom after the death of Mufasa), defeat him, regain his throne, and re-establish order in his kingdom once again. He did all of this, and in doing so he saved his realm from tyranny and oppression. We all must do that in our own lives! How often are our lives in disarray when there's something we could be doing about it? How often do we fall short of our potential because we forget who we really are as children of God? The Kingdom of God is not absent from us, you see. It is we who are absent from it. We are typically too preoccupied with our false selves to see that the Kingdom of Heaven is at hand. It is all around us and within us, but we're blind to it until we're born again.... and again, and again, and again on a daily basis. But when we take up our crosses daily, re-centering ourselves in God, then we see. There's more to us than meets the eye, and there's more to reality than what we perceive as reality. Indeed, we are each a microcosm of the Macrocosm; and the whole of creation is sacred. It's all holy ground. "As above, so below", as the old hermetic axiom goes. But understanding this reality takes time, practice, patience, and obedience to the Spirit.

The Lion King is clearly a story of transformation wherein the light conquers the darkness and good is victorious over evil. It is a creative retelling of the ancient Osiris myth. Osiris is slain by his evil brother, Typhon, who then usurps the throne and rules as a despot until Horus, the son of Osiris and the rightful heir to the throne, returns to defeat Typhon and regain his rightful claim to the throne. It's a tale as old as time, and it's the truest kind of story in an archetypal, psychological, spiritual sense. You see this same allegory played out in Harry Potter and the Chamber of Secrets, the ancient tale of Orpheus descending into the underworld to rescue Eurydice, and many other stories. Beauty and the Beast is yet another story about transformation. It beautifully illustrates a necessary change of heart which we must all undergo; death to an old way of being and resurrection into a new way of being and seeing. It is yet another tale in which love eventually conquers all. But you see all of this portrayed in the gospel story more powerfully than anywhere else. Jesus descends into the grave, emerges resurrected, and then he defeats the ultimate villain: death itself. And he not only defeated death for himself, but he defeated it for the whole of humanity. And he did it without violence! His entire life story is an expression of God's tireless, outpouring, unconditional love for humanity. Jesus is the archetypal Hero of all heroes! That's why his story is the greatest story ever told. It's the greatest because it's the truest. It's profoundly and timeless true from start to finish. It is not merely a myth. It's not a meaningless fable, not just a fairytale, and not merely a pretty story. It is a story that points to a reality more real than what we commonly perceive to be reality. It gives us a glimpse at the meta-reality that gives meaning to our material reality. It is a glimpse at the Truth in the deepest, most eternal sense. The kind of Truth that is truer than fact.

The character of God is revealed to us in Christ, and being a Christian is about trusting in God by following Christ. Thus, to love God you must love what God loves: the world! Since God is within us all, you love God by loving your neighbor as yourself. That's why the Greatest Commandment is to love God with all your heart, might, mind and strength; and the second greatest commandment is like unto it, that you should love your neighbor as yourself. The body of Christ is composed of the entire human family, you see; and that is why Jesus said, "If ye have done it unto the least of these, my brethren, ye have done it unto me." That's the heart of Christianity as I see it. It's about being reborn into a new way of seeing the world, which results in a new way of living in it. A way in which you become an instrument of the Holy Spirit. A way of seeing and living that is centered in Christ, seeing God in all and all in God, with an understanding that all human beings are brothers and sisters under the fatherhood of Him. When you become intuitively aware of this reality, you see God in the face of the beggar on the street and all people whom you meet; and you'll treat them as extensions of yourself, for so they are.

This panentheistic way of seeing, which sees God in all and all in God, is at the very heart of nearly every mystical tradition. You can find it in Christianity, Judaism, Hinduism, and Buddhism, for example. It's amazing to see that the mystics of all the world's religions will tend to agree on most things, whereas the fundamentalists of different religions will often disagree to the point of killing each other. This is because mystics derive their understanding of God from direct experience, whereas fundamentalists derive their concepts of God from the stories and traditions of their respective cultures; which they tend to take too literally. The former has a first-hand knowledge of God, whereas the latter has a second-hand knowledge of God. Mystics of all cultures tend to agree with one another because they've all experienced the same God, though they all have their own respective names and concepts for Him. Since they've all had some experience of the infinitely Ineffable Mystery that is God, knowing well that no finite concepts of God can ever suffice to accurately describe Him, they don't fuss over the details in the way that fundamentalists do. They know that there's really just one infinite God, though He has been given countless names by countless cultures throughout the ages; and they know that no finite person or book can claim to have an infallible monopoly on the Truth as it pertains to Him. Every religious myth on earth is a particular culture's best attempt at describing the indescribable. All of our concepts of God are symbolic attempts at making the ineffable effable.

Our respective religious traditions are lenses through which we see reality, but those lenses do not give us perfect vision. St Paul, who was a mystic of the first magnitude, summed this up beautifully when he said, "for now we see through a glass, darkly; but then face to face: now I know in part; but then shall I know even as also I am known." (1 Corinthians 13:12) Whether we are Catholics, Methodists,

Mormons, or Muslims, our respective religious traditions are imperfect lenses by which we peer into the mystery of God's perfection. All Mystics know this, and thus they are content to humbly work in their respective traditions while realizing that God is infinitely more than any tradition can fully divulge. Mystery of all mysteries, we all understand and misunderstand God in our own respective ways. But whereas mystics from various traditions tend to agree that God is beyond our concepts which we attribute to Him, fundamentalists will fight tooth and nail over whose concept of God is right. That's why faith rooted in dogma looks very different from faith rooted in spiritual experience.

Mystical (i.e. spiritual) experiences, or experiences of the Sacred, are very real. They have occurred in every age and culture from time immemorial. There are scores of people from various religious traditions who have experienced mystical unions with God, whether only once or many times during their lives. They afterwards try to share their insights with other people to the best of their abilities, but they are generally misunderstood by all except those who have had similar experiences. This kind of experience is what I call an inner initiation. An awakening of the Soul. Sudden Enlightenment, or Sartori, as it is known in the Zen Buddhist tradition. It's when belief transforms into an inexplicable, intuitive kind of knowing. Gnosis. Usually less dramatic than what happened to Paul on the road to Damascus, people tend to come away from these transcendental experiences with a new way of seeing reality. A worldview of indivisible unity and panentheism, in which God is in all and all are in God. A worldview in which your "I" begins to look more like "we." It's a diminution of your egoic persona and an augmentation, or amplification, of the Logos persona within you. The Christ persona, of which body you are a part. This is what I believe John the Baptist meant when he said about the Lord, "He must increase, but I must decrease." To be born again, we must surrender to a plan greater than our own, God's plan, and allow ourselves to be instruments for the Great Work of that plan. Being born again means less of me working in the world, and more of the Holy Spirit working through me in the world. That is the Way of the Heart, the way of the cross, the way of death and rebirth, and the foundation of the mystical or contemplative life.

Mystical experience is simply a term to describe any first-hand experience of the Spirit, which is a mystery. Mystics are people who have mystical experiences or visions, and they will often keep it to themselves for a number of reasons. One reason being that they are humble and don't want to boast, another reason being that they want to avoid casting pearls before swine only to be ostracized or persecuted by those who wouldn't understand, another reason being that they know not to tell people certain truths until they're ready to receive them, and yet another reason being that what they experienced is simply beyond words. Unutterable and unlawful to be told. One example of this can be found in Paul's second epistle to the Corinthians, wherein he talks about the mystical experience of a "man in Christ" whom he wouldn't name.

He said, *"Though there is nothing to be gained by it, I will go on to visions and revelations of the Lord. I know a man in Christ who fourteen years ago was caught up to the third heaven – whether in the body or out of the body I do not know, God knows. And I know that this man was caught up into paradise – whether in the body or out of the body I do not know, God knows – and he heard things that cannot be told, which man may not utter. On behalf of this man I will boast, but on my own behalf I will not boast, except of my weaknesses – though if I should wish to boast, I would not be a fool, for I would be speaking the truth; but I refrain from it, so that no one may think more of me than he sees in me or hears from me."* (2 Corinthians 12: 1-6)

It seems probable to me that he was talking about himself; though it is possible that he was talking about a friend who had discreetly entrusted him with the details of a very profound mystical experience.

Examples of mystical experiences abound in the Bible, and millions of people all over the world have had them. Some people have them frequently. This is why I have no problem seeing the stories in the Bible as being divinely inspired. I have no doubt that many of those stories were penned by people who have had profound mystical experiences, and those experiences inspired them to share their insights in the form of allegory. And some of those stories undoubtedly developed organically over hundreds, if not thousands, of years. Rather than being the sole creation of any one person, it is likely that many Bible stories were once oral traditions inspired by the collective experiences of an entire culture. Folklore handed down orally from one generation to another until eventually being written down long after their original inception. Such is the case with many of the world's greatest myths, I think. They are ancient, archetypal narratives from the collective unconscious of humanity, inspired by mankind's mystical experiences over countless ages of time.

It may well be that the mystical myths of the ancient world are encoded into our DNA, having been passed down to us in our genes over millennia throughout the process of human evolution. Perhaps that's why they are so powerful. When we hear archetypal myths, it's as if we somehow remember ancient memories of a primordial nature. Memories that the human species has collectively retained as it has evolved over thousands of years. One might argue that the process of evolution is a mystical unfolding of consciousness on a massive scale, experiencing and expressing itself in increasingly greater complexity over time. From this mystical standpoint, creation was not a one-time event. Creation is always happening. God is always creating. Always becoming. This endless cycle of creation, which we might as well call evolution, is a mystical experience felt by the whole of nature. We can see this on a small scale in our own lives. We evolve, or transform, into better versions of ourselves as we learn and grow over time. We grow wiser with each new insight we glean from life experiences, and we are changed a little bit by each experience. What could be more mystical than that? It's not supernatural. It's just perfectly natural. We live in a God-soaked universe, as Richard Rohr would say. Every day-to-day experience can be seen as a mystical experience, but only if you're present enough to see the divine working within the mundane. Only if you're present enough to see that time and space are just transient expressions of the timeless, spaceless, infinite reality that is God.

Mystical experiences are gifts of grace. They are little moments of clarity in which a small corner of the veil is lifted, allowing you to perceive deeper into the mystery of God. Such experiences are very humbling, for they show you just how little you actually know. Indeed, they show to you just how little you are capable of knowing. They leave you with a sense of wonder, gratitude, openness, humility, and useful emptiness. By being emptied of preconceived notions and culturally inherited concepts about what God is like, you then have a bit more room in your mind for God to show you what He is like. These little moments of clarity and insight can be brought about by centering prayer and meditation.

In the Buddhist tradition, there are two kinds of mystics or "contemplatives". The first kind is the Bodhicitta and the other is the Bodhisattva. Both have experienced the Sacred, but the difference between the two lies in what they respectively choose to do with the insight or knowledge gleaned from their spiritual experiences. The Bodhicitta retreats from the world, usually moving away from civilization to live in a monastery or a small shack out in the wilderness. They strive to spend as much time as possible in a state of tranquility and spiritual ecstasy, present to the infinite but absent to the finite. But the Bodhisattva delves deeper into the world of everyday life, laboring alongside and sharing the burdens of his fellow men, attempting to share his light with them via action. The former is an enlightened man who hides his light under a bushel, and the latter is an enlightened man who sets his light on a candle stick for all to enjoy.

Just as the scientist who wishes to change the world will make active use of his discoveries rather than keeping his eye constantly buried in the microscope, the mystic who wishes to make a difference in the world will learn to live in awareness of the spiritual plane without withdrawing from activity in the physical plane.

"We must work the works of Him who sent me while it is day; night is coming, when no one can work." (John 9:4)

The object of contemplative life, a life in awareness of the Spirit, is to bear forth the fruits of the Spirit in day to day life. As Paul said in his epistle to the Galatians, "the fruit of the Spirit is love, joy, peace, patience, kindness, goodness, faithfulness, gentleness, and self-control." (Gal 5:22-23)

What does it profit us to know and not do? No employer hires you for what you know. He hires you for what you can do. He hires you for the skills and services you can offer which will enhance his business. So it is with life. Merely knowing about God doesn't make us very useful to God. Showing forth our knowledge of God by actively exemplifying His love to others in daily life is what makes us useful to God. If we've been graced with experiences of His divine love and grace, it's because He wants us to extend that love and grace to our fellow man. He wants us to be instruments of that love and grace. Instruments of the Spirit.

"Many cry to the Lord that they may win riches, that they may avoid losses; they cry that their family may be established, they ask for temporal happiness, for worldly dignities; and, lastly, they cry for bodily health, which is the patrimony of the poor. For these and suchlike things many cry to the Lord; hardly one cries for the Lord Himself! How easy it is for a man to desire all manner of things from the Lord and yet not desire the Lord Himself! As though the gift could be sweeter than the Giver!" — St Thomas Aquinas, *On Prayer and the Contemplative Life.*

Centering prayer is not like the kind of prayer in which you ask God for things. Too many people today think that prayer is about treating God as if He were a cosmic genie who exists to grant our wishes. That's not what prayer is about. As Jesus said, God already knows what you need before you ask Him. So, what is prayer for then? To re-center you in God. To align your will with His. More often than not prayer is not so much about speaking to God, but about listening to Him! It's about saying, "Here am I, Lord. What would you have me do?" It's about tuning out of the frequency of worldly distractions, tuning in to the frequency of God, and harmonizing your life thereby. That's what St Paul meant when he told the Thessalonians to "pray without ceasing." He certainly didn't mean that you should go around reciting the Lord's Prayer or the Our Father all day every day. It's about being silent and still, having your heart constantly open to receive instruction from the Holy Spirit. That's mysticism in its purest and most basic form. That's how to have a first-hand, experiential, personal relationship with God. Be still and know that He is God. Stop talking long enough to hear Him speak. He's always speaking, though most people aren't listening. He speaks through all the varied actions and laws of nature, and He speaks with the voice of your own conscience. A mystical experience isn't always a huge, mind-blowing, revelatory experience. More often than not, it's a subtle experience; and being down-to-earth will produce more of these experiences than having your head in the clouds will. Whereas meditation often involves visualization and imagination, contemplation simply involves observing what is. It's about being fully present in the moment, wherever it is that you happen to be, doing whatever it is that you happen to be doing.

In the words of the late Father Thomas Keating, a wise and insightful teacher of contemplative practice, "a mystic is not a special kind of person; each person is a special kind of mystic." God is present in all, and He is speaking to all. Question is, are we listening? If someone can't find God, it's likely because they aren't truly looking for Him. There's something else they desire more, whatever that may be. If someone can't perceive God speaking to them, it's because they're not truly interested in hearing what He has to say. There's something else in which they're more interested, whatever that may be. "Blessed are the pure in heart, for they shall see God" (Matthew 5:8) If you wish to find God, your heart must be pure. That is, God must be the ultimate object of your heart's desire. Your desire to know God must be greater than your desire for material wealth, sensual pleasure, adventure, social status or anything else. Your desire to know God must even be greater than your desire to for food, drink, clothing, shelter and general sustenance. Seek God first, and the rest will fall into place.

"Therefore, take no thought, saying, What shall we eat? or, What shall we drink? or, Wherewithal shall we be clothed? For after all these things do the Gentiles seek: for your heavenly Father knoweth that ye have need of all these things. But seek ye first the kingdom of God, and his righteousness; and all these things shall be added unto you." (Matt 6:31-33) "Ask, and it shall be given you; seek, and ye shall find; knock, and it shall be opened unto you: For everyone that asketh receiveth; and he that seeketh findeth; and to him that knocketh it shall be opened." (Matthew 7:7-8)

In conclusion, we need to get back to the contemplative heart of Christianity. We need to make more room for mysticism. More Christians need to learn about exegesis, hermeneutics and epistemology so that they can savor the inner truths of the scriptures rather than stumble on the outer symbols that esoterically allude to them. We need to realize that the Bible is not a book, but rather a library of various books written in a variety of literary styles. Some of it is history, some of it is myth, some of it is poetry, and some of it is prose; but it's all true! We need to get away from the modern mentality that sees myth as being merely fiction. It's far more than fiction! It's often truer than fact!

Myths are far more sophisticated than most people realize. As I hope I've successfully demonstrated in this article, they can have innumerable layers of meaning. I've heard some people, typically individuals who have become disenchanted with organized religion, insist that the story of Christ is just a myth; as if a myth is merely meaningless fiction. And I've even heard some say that Christianity is just a rebranded form of pagan sun-worship. Solar mythology. They see some astrotheology in it, so they quickly jump to the conclusion that there's nothing more to it than that. This line of thinking takes too literally the words of Tertulian when he said, "You say we worship the sun; so do you." Is there some solar symbolism in the Bible? Absolutely. It's no coincidence that Jesus had twelve disciples, that he rose again on the third day, and that his birthday has been traditionally accepted as December 25th; just a few days after the Winter Solstice. Anyone who understands the zodiac and the precession of the equinoxes will immediately see solar and stellar correspondences in the gospel narrative and other bible stories. But there's far more to those stories than anthropomorphic retellings of astronomical phenomenon. The astronomical and astrological correspondences to those stories are symbolic in nature. They are deliberate details that add more meaning to the allegory, but they do not make up the Big Picture of it. Rather, they are added layers of symbolism that further allude to the Big Picture. Was there a lot of solar symbolism in ancient pagan religions? Of course. Apollo was an indeed anthropomorphic solar figure. But the fact of the matter is that the wisest pagans have never worshipped the Sun as the infinite Creator. Rather, they saw it as a finite metaphor representing the infinite attributes of God. Rightfully so, I might add. Seeing as how God has always been figuratively associated with light, what other natural object could be more fitting than the sun as a metaphor for the illuminating, life-giving benevolence of God? While Jesus can indeed be seen as a solar figure to a certain extent, that's not all he is. He's much more than that. The sun gives light to the world in a literal sense, but Jesus is the Light of the World in a much deeper way; and the sun in the sky is better seen as a metaphor for Christ rather than the other way around.

If you hadn't noticed, this problematic tendency to interpret things too literally has not only crept into our religious denominations, but also into our Commanderies of Masonic Knights Templar. I've met some Sir Knights in our Order who naively believe that Freemasonry and Masonic Templary can be traced to the medieval Knights Templar! I'm sorry to burst our brothers' bubbles, but there is zero evidence to suggest that we have any authentic, historical connection to those crusading warrior monks. We merely pay homage to the chivalric virtues and warrior spirit of Templary, waging no holy wars and fighting no crusades except those which are to be fought within ourselves! Besides, if we were indeed descended from those original monastic knights, they'd be rolling in their graves to know that their modern-day successors have devolved into what the Order of the Temple has become in most Commanderies: a social club for Christian Masons who occasionally gather to read the minutes, pay the bills, raise a bit of money for the Knights Templar Eye Foundation, and practice drill and ceremony while wearing superfluously ostentatious regalia.

We must remember the initiatic purpose of the Commandery as a Masonic body. As Albert Pike so eloquently wrote, the purpose of Freemasonry is to facilitate "a continuous advance, by means of the instruction contained in a series of Degrees, toward the Light, by the elevation of the Celestial, the Spiritual, and the Divine, over the Earthly, Sensual, Material, and Human, in the Nature of Man." The Masonic Knights Templar share that same purpose! As with all other degrees in all Rites of Masonry, the three Chivalric Orders of the Commandery are intended to help our Brothers continue their journey in search of more light; but this time in a Christian context! The Blue Degrees deal with the search and substitute for the Word, the Capitular Degrees culminate in the discovery of the Word, and the Cryptic Degrees present an allegory explaining the preservation of the Word; but the Commandery Orders illustrate a new perspective on meaning of the Word. They point to Christ as the incarnation of the Word! The Word made flesh! The Word that in the beginning was with God, and was God. Whereas Freemasonry in general is about illumination, Masonic Templary is about Christian illuminism. Just like we are speculative Masons who use the jargon and symbolism of architecture for more noble and glorious purposes than the operative Masons of old, we are likewise speculative Knights who use the themes and symbols of Chivalry for more noble and glorious purposes than the operative Knights of old. As speculative Masons, we are not literally building any physical temples. Rather, we are building an upright life erected to God. Similarly, as Masonic Templars, we are not literally fighting any external enemies of the Christian faith. Rather, we are fighting internal enemies; defending the faith from the ruffians and infidels within our own hearts. These inner enemies are pride, lust, greed, selfishness, hatred, bigotry, racism, intolerance, ignorance, superstition, fanaticism, tyranny, despair, apathy, envy, condescension, vanity, anger, fear, etc. and etc. When you interpret the allegorical legends of our Masonic Rites and Chivalric Orders literally, you deprive yourself of their deeper meaning and you miss out on the transformation which they are intended to facilitate within you.

Indeed, excessive literalism has caused a lot of trouble in the world; and it continues to do so. The pages of history have been hideously stained by blood due to well-meaning people interpreting the Bible and other holy books too literally. Scores of people have been hurt and even killed by religious fanatics over mere differences of opinion. Just look at the gruesome horrors of the Spanish Inquisition, where Christians tortured and killed people merely for saying or believing things that the Church declared to be heretical! Look at Islamic extremism, where an overly literalistic understanding of jihad has led some fundamentalist Muslims to commit despicable acts of terrorism! Look at how the Bible has been deplorably used to condone racism and slavery! Horrendous injustices can be, and often are, caused by excessively literalistic interpretations of religious texts. Such are the dangers of fundamentalism and religious legalism, which can typically result in bigotry and fanaticism rather than enlightenment. And in addition to people hurting each other, people have also harmed the planet because of their literalistic understanding of the creation myth as told in Genesis. Think about how differently people would treat mother nature if they didn't interpret the book of Genesis so literally. There are many Christians who think that all animals and plant life are here for us to use and abuse as we see fit. That mindset has had disastrous effects on the environment. Also, just think how different the lives of Christians would look if they were to realize that Christianity isn't just about believing in Jesus so that they can get into Heaven after they die. If they would realize that it's mostly about discipleship, which is a lifestyle devoted to following Jesus, a life centered in God, there would be a lot more kindness and compassion in the world and a lot less injustice. Christianity would be far more attractive to far more people if more Christians were actually disciples of Christ, for it would be a far more loving and inclusive tradition than what we have allowed it to become in many of our churches and communities. With that in mind, I shall end this article with a quote from Jesus. He didn't say that men would know you to be a Christian because you wear a cross around your neck, sit on the front row at church, and loudly profess your faith for all to hear. No, indeed.

Jesus said, "by this all people will know that you are my disciples, if you have love for one another." (John 13:35)

Sources/Recommended Reading:

"Aeion" by Carl Jung
"Confessions" by St Augustine

"The Cloud of Unknowing" by Anonymous
"The Heart of Christianity" by Marcus Borg
"Hero With A Thousand Faces" by Joseph Campbell
"The Holy Bible"
"Inner Christianity" by Richard Smoley
"Invitation to Love" by Thomas Keating
"Jung on Mythology" by Carl Jung
Edited by Robert A. Segal
"Maps of Meaning" by Jordan Peterson
"Mere Christianity" by C. S. Lewis "Myths to Live By" by Joseph Campbell
"On Prayer and the Contemplative Life" by St Thomas Aquinas
"Reading the Bible Again for the First Time" by Marcus Borg
"Summa Theologica", Volume I & II by St Thomas Aquinas
""Universal Christ" by Richard Rohr
"Wherever You Go, There You Are" By Jon Kabat-Zinn

Freemasonry the Verb
By Michael R. Poll

Let's take a look at us, the whole of Freemasonry —
who are we, what are we, and why is there even a need for
an organization like Freemasonry. I believe that the best way
to try and understand who and what we are is to go back to
the past. I don't mean the early days of Speculative
Freemasonry. I also don't mean to the days of the old
Operative Freemasons. I mean to an earlier time. I'd like us
to go back to a period of time known as the Dark Ages.

The Dark Ages are known as a time of general
ignorance for most of Europe. This time is called the Dark
Ages because, generally speaking, dark is considered the
opposite of light, or enlightenment. People during this time
were anything but enlightened. There is a thought that the
overall ignorance of the people during this time was not by
choice, but by plan. It's believed by some that there was a
policy by the Kings, emperors, and maybe even the church
to purposely keep the masses ignorant. It was felt that an
uneducated population was far easier to control that an
educated population.

Free expression was simply not allowed during the
Dark Ages. Education was not allowed. Voicing opinions or
beliefs that were different from those who were in charge
could result in imprisonment. There was only one thought,
one opinion, or one belief that was allowed. That was the
opinion, thought, or belief of whoever was in charge — the
church, King, or Emperor. If you had any opinion or belief
that was different from whoever was in charge, you had
better keep it to yourself. Only one opinion was allowed and
if you were not the one in charge, you had better openly
agree with the opinion you were given.

One of the common symbols of Freemasonry today is
the Bible. On the altars of our lodges we find the Bible.
When our lodges are at labor and open, so is the Bible open.

We sometimes forget, don't think about, or may not even know the significance of the Bible being open on our altars. The simple fact is that you can't read a closed Bible. In order to read the Bible, and know what's in it, you have to open it. That is exactly what was *not wanted* during the Dark Ages. During that time, for those few who could even read, the Bible was not allowed to be read. You did not find a Bible open — except maybe in church. If you wanted to know what was inside the Bible, you asked your priest. He would tell you what was inside the Bible. You would not be allowed to find that out for yourself. The reason would seem simple, if you read the Bible you may understand it in a different way then you were told. That was the last thing that was wanted.

It was a time that can be considered as the time of one. Again, there was only one thought, one opinion, or one belief that was allowed. That was the opinion, thought, or belief of whoever was in charge — the church, King, or Emperor. This is why the Bible is open on our lodge altars. The Bible is there for you to read, understand, and decide for yourself what it means.

During the Dark Ages if you expressed an opinion or belief different than the one that was allowed, you simply went to prison or were executed. Actually, during that time, being executed may have been the more humane punishment. The prisons were extraordinarily unpleasant.

But while it was possible to control unwanted opinions and beliefs that were spoken, it was *not* possible to control, or even know about, what someone was thinking. The policy of one could not affect what individuals thought. It was a time when there were no televisions, Internet or cell phones with which someone could entertain themselves. For entertainment, people often when outside, sat under a tree and thought about things. They would think about anything and everything. It was here that this policy of one began to fall apart.

Because there was no way to control what someone thought, individuals began to think about many things, imagine new concepts and ideas and yet act like they're only thought was the one given to them by whoever was in charge. The problem for those thinking these wonderful new ideas was that they had no one to share these new ideas with. These new ideas began to bubble up in the people and since humans are social creatures, it became increasingly difficult to keep these secret thoughts to themselves. What happened next changed the world.

The people who would sit around and think of wonderful ideas simply had to do something with these ideas. They had to share them with someone. It would seem logical that when they did, it would most likely be a family member or close friend that they could trust, but it seemed inevitable that they would end up sharing their thoughts and ideas with someone.

Of course, they would explain that what they wanted to tell was a secret and if the secrecy were violated, they could get in a great deal of trouble. They would tell the secret ideas to the other and then something amazing would often happen. Many times, the one being told the secret idea would return the favor to tell his own secret idea, maybe as payment for sharing with him.

So, think about it, where originally you had two people each with one idea, now you have two people each with two new ideas. Both of them benefited by the sharing of ideas. That was a good thing for both of them. That was a particularly important and desirable thing for them.

After a while, little groups were formed. Maybe a half a dozen or so individuals were sworn to secrecy. When they all started telling their private thoughts and ideas, everyone in the group benefited. They found this to be an extremely good thing. They were educating themselves and expanding their thoughts and ideas. They were very well aware that what they were doing was against the law, but they were also aware that it was absolutely necessary for them to do this in order to grow as human beings.

These little groups met in secret, taught each other in secret, and helped each other become better than they were before. It was the seed that would one day grow into what we know today as Speculative Freemasonry. Of course, this is speculation, but it is born out of logic and a study of human nature. If you see someone sitting in a chair and the next time you see him, he is standing outside, you can assume that at some point he got up and walked outside.

Make no mistake, what these little groups were doing in secret during the Dark Ages was exactly what is natural for humans to do. You cannot forcibly keep humans ignorant forever. Our minds are private and while it is possible for us to be deceived and believe things that are just not so, we are mentally capable of sooner or later discovering the truth. The growth of our minds will not be denied.

Little intellectual study groups, over time, eventually developed into Speculative Freemasonry. They were not an entertainment club or a social group, they were individuals on a true mission. They were doing something important.

In those early days, Freemasonry, and the groups from which it evolved, was a verb, an action. Freemasonry was doing something. It was providing an education that was found nowhere else. Stop and think for a minute. You can get in your car today and drive down any street you choose. You will probably pass more than a few churches of all different faiths. They are all there clearly identifying themselves with signs saying, "Here I am, this is what we teach, this is what we believe." They are not hiding. They are very much in the open. Children are today not denied education, it's just the opposite. Children are required by law to go to school and learn all of the things that were denied by law during the Dark Ages.

Yes, we have many problems in this world. The country is politically divided, but we are not be stood against a wall and executed simply because we express an opinion different than our leaders. We will not be imprisoned because we express a different religious belief or that we seek to learn or have ideas of science, medicine or pretty much anything else that is different. We have a freedom today that those during the Dark Ages could scarcely imagine.

Very early Speculative Freemasonry was in an actual war against ignorance. In many areas, they met in secret because to be open about what they were doing, and teaching would mean imprisonment. The work that they were doing was dead serious. They were teaching humanity. They were giving their members the opportunity to grow, to learn and experience things that they would find nowhere else.

Do you see why Freemasonry became so popular and spread so quickly to all corners of the world? Do you see why dictators and those who sought to rule by oppression saw Freemasonry as the enemy? The truth is that Freemasonry has always been the enemy of ignorance.

Freemasonry was an active Order, on an actual mission and it was winning the war against ignorance. We know that the United States was not created by Freemasonry, but certainly Freemasons had a hand in its creation. Certainly, the teachings of Freemasonry played a role in the formation of our government. We were the New Atlantis.

But at that time, there was more that was happening with Freemasonry and the world. Simply put, Freemasonry won the war. Of course, ignorance was not gone from the world, but tremendous, good changes were made. Freemasonry did play a leading role in that change. And when Freemasonry did win this war on organized ignorance, there came something else that we may overlook.

Think about it. If you work and work for a very long time on one goal, such as replacing darkness with light, and this long, hard work succeeds and you achieve your goals, what comes next? Remember, Freemasonry was not a club, it was an active order with a very real and serious purpose. Freemasonry was a place of education. The reason it existed was to give the world something that it did not have, something that was very much needed.

The work Freemasonry was doing was also outlawed in many areas. As a result, there was a tremendous bond created between the Masons and the work that they were doing for all humanity. Bringing light, education, to those who needed light was the sole reason for the existence of Speculative Freemasonry.

But once they won that war, and did what they had been trying for so very long to do, what was next for them? What role would they play after they actually achieved what they had been trying to achieve for so very long? That's the question that they faced.

The creation of the United States can be seen as the crowning glory of the work of Freemasonry. Freedom of thought, expression and education was woven into fabric of the young United States. Let's take a look at what was happening.

When the United States was created, people living here were cut off politically from England. It was necessary for them to form a new government. The government that they created was based on individual, sovereign states organizing themselves under a central federal government. It was a bold and new concept for a government.

But just as it was necessary for the young country to create a government for itself, it was necessary for Freemasonry to reorganize in the new country. Freemasonry that existed in the 13 colonies prior to the revolution existed under the Grand Lodges of England, Ireland and Scotland. Provincial Grand Lodges had been created in the colonies to supervise Freemasonry. But once independence for the United States had been achieved, these Provincial Grand Lodges dissolved themselves.

Just as it was necessary for the young United States to organize itself into a government, so was it necessary for Freemasonry to reorganize. There was talk in the early days that maybe Freemasonry in the United States should organize itself as Freemasonry in Europe. Maybe they should have one Grand Lodge for the whole of the United States. There was even talk of George Washington becoming the first Grand Master of the Grand Lodge of the United States.

But after further talk and thought, the Masons came up with a different idea. Since states' rights was such an important and unique concept of the young United States, maybe Freemasonry should follow the model already created. Maybe Freemasonry in the United States should organize with one Grand Lodge in each state rather than one for the whole United States. They seemed to like that idea and developed it a little further.

After some discussion, they settled on having one Grand Lodge per state, one language per Grand Lodge — English, and one ritual per state, and that would develop into the ritual commonly known as the American rite or the Webb ritual. Remember that Concept of One that created so many problems in the Dark Ages?

I can't get into the minds of the early Freemasons in the United States. I don't know why they felt the need to develop this Concept of One. I don't know why they felt the need for every lodge, every Grand Lodge and every Mason to be alike. The simple fact is that we are not all alike and its nonsense to think that we are or can be. We all have our own likes, dislikes, strengths, and weaknesses. That's normal. But it seems that the early Masons in the United States wanted all of Masonry in our young country to be alike.

Of course, then there was Louisiana. The fly in the ointment. The Territory of Louisiana achieved statehood in 1812. That same year the Grand Lodge of Louisiana was created.

The Grand Lodge located itself in New Orleans. The city of New Orleans was a valuable port that connected the Gulf of Mexico with the rest of the United States. It was far cheaper to ship goods down the Mississippi River to the port of New Orleans and out to the Gulf of Mexico than to try to move goods by pack train through the woods of the undeveloped country.

Along with the crews that travelled to New Orleans were a fair share of Freemasons.

As Masons do when they visit a new city, they wanted to visit Lodges in New Orleans. They were in for a shock.

Within just a few years of the development of the Grand Lodge of Louisiana, the lodges under its jurisdiction were working in 5 different languages: French, English, Spanish, Italian and German. In addition, at least three rituals were being work: York or American Webb, Scottish Rite, and French or Modern Rite. The visiting Masons had no idea what they were experiencing. It was different. It was *not* to their liking.

By the mid 1800's, the dislike for the *different* Louisiana Masonry grew hostile and a second Grand Lodge was created with the goal of forcing Louisiana Freemasonry to be a copy of Masonry as worked in the rest of the US. While this effort to change the nature of Masonry in Louisiana was not completely successful, it does stand as an example of the determination for the Concept of One attitude that had developed in the United States.

So, we had two situations happening around the same time in Freemasonry around the world. In Europe, Freemasonry was trying to find its new role in the world since its former role as a warrior of the enlightenment was no longer needed. While in the young United States, Freemasonry was adopting the impossible policy of trying to make every Lodge into a clone of the other. What would the future bring? And that all brings us to today.

In the United States today (and, so I am told, in other areas of the world), Freemasonry too many times resembles a second-rate social club rather than a center of education. Our transformation from an active Order to a pseudo-club seems complete. Our meetings too often are limited to a meal downstairs, opening the Lodge, reading the minutes, paying the bills, and then maybe a little discussion on who is sick and any upcoming barbecues or social events. That's it. In far too many cases, the Lodge experience is void of any education at all.

When members became bored with what we offered, they began seeking entertainment elsewhere, they stopped attending meetings or left us. When our numbers dropped to the point that lodges began closing and others found it difficult to pay bills, many lodges began dropping standards as to who they would admit. It was a vicious cycle.

The lack of education as to who we are combined with taking anyone who paid the fees to join seemed to be the death blow for Freemasonry. But then something odd began happening. Young Masons joining us wanted, demanded, the return of Freemasonry from many, many years ago. They wanted the education, the esoteric philosophy, and the action that once defined us. They wanted Freemasonry the Verb.

Today, we're seeing an almost war within Freemasonry. We see some with the club mentality who have been around long enough that they have worked themselves into leadership positions. For too many of them, Freemasonry is a means for feeding their ego. They like the grand sounding titles, the authority, and respect that they tell themselves they have. They have the twisted idea that Freemasonry is some grand club designed to make the unworthy feel worthy simply through membership. They hold onto their paper kingdoms with a tight grip and will do anything at all, including destroying Freemasonry itself, before relinquishing the power that they believe they have.

And then you have the young Masons. They are satisfied with nothing but the teachings that they know are hidden away in our symbols and philosophy. They know that rank and office mean responsibility, not empty power. They will accept nothing but true Freemasonry.

So, what will the future be? I believe we will end up with a bright future. Freemasonry is once again becoming a verb. But this time, it's fighting what it has become. Freemasonry is fighting elements within Freemasonry. It is fighting itself to save itself. I do not believe that it will be an easy fight. Some are willing to do almost anything to hold onto their ego fueled bases of power. But I see a light at the end of the tunnel.

There is a power within Freemasonry. Counterfeit Freemasons do not possess this power. The power they possess is empty. Little by little Freemasonry is again winning another war. This one is against the ignorance that was allowed to take control of Freemasonry itself.

I believe we will see in the next years amazing things and in the end a return to true and pure Freemasonry.

The Battle of New Orleans & Freemasonry
By Michael R. Poll

A few years ago, Brother Pete Norman invited me to be the Anson Jones Lecturer for the Scottish Rite Valley of Houston. It was quite an honor and privilege. When I arrived, Brother Pete drove me around the area on a tour of the various sites of interest. One of those sites was Holland Lodge No. 1. That was of particular significance to me as a Louisiana Mason. Not only was John Henry Holland a Past Grand Master of the Grand Lodge of Louisiana (more times than anyone else), but he was also the founder and first Worshipful Master of my Mother Lodge, Friends of Harmony No. 58. Sadly, much of the very colorful early history of Brother John Holland seems lost in time. So much, for example, of his actions and activity around the time of the founding of the Grand Lodge of Texas is unknown. Too many records were simply lost or destroyed. Coincidentally, not long ago I visited Humble Cottage Lodge No. 19 in Opelousas, Louisiana. Brother James "Buddy" Pearce, the lodge secretary, told me an interesting story about Humble Cottage Lodge and the founding of the Grand Lodge of Texas. He claimed that when Grand Master John Holland gave the warrant for the founding for the first Lodge in Texas, a natural stop for the brother delivering the warrant would be Opelousas. He said that Opelousas was one of the common routes from Louisiana to Texas. He also claimed that while the records of the Lodge were destroyed long ago, he feels that it would be likely that the brother would have visited Humble Cottage during his rest stop. I have no way of knowing if this story is correct or not, but it does seem possible. And this is the problem with so much of early Louisiana Masonic history. So many of our early records have been destroyed and far too much of our early history is relegated to legend and lore. This is what I will discuss a bit in this paper, legend and lore. Some of it we know to be fact, but other aspects simply cannot be proven. The problem for historians is that because we know certain things did happen, but cannot prove how or why they happened, we cannot discount logical rumors or unsubstantiated accounts of events.

Let's look at a rather famous event in Louisiana history. The Battle of New Orleans is one of the most written about, talked about, and even sang about events in the history of Louisiana. This battle was the final battle in the so-called War of 1812 between the United States and England. This war is sometimes known as the second battle of independence for the United States. We also know that this final battle was about as decisive an American victory as possible and most likely propelled the commander of the American forces, Andrew Jackson, into the presidency of the United States. I grew up not far from where that battle took place. All through my childhood years, I remember visiting the Chalmette Battlefield and seeing both the raised embankment behind which the American forces fought and a large open field where so many of the British marched to their deaths. Also growing up, I remember being puzzled by many of the books that I read on this battle. While the overall outcome of the battle in all the books was the same, many of the important details were different and sometimes contradictory. I should also point out that these books were written by individuals who were considered competent historians. I began to realize that this battle had reached the level of legend since much of what was identified as "facts" was exaggerations or outright made up accounts of the events. I set upon a goal of trying to understand what actually happened during that battle, before and after it, to see if I could discover anything different about what might have happened in such a historic and legendary battle.

Most accounts of the battle itself generally agree with the overall details. Maj. Gen. Andrew Jackson was given command of the American forces with the goal of defending New Orleans from a British attack believed to be impending. Jackson set up a defensive line about five miles outside of

New Orleans at the Chalmette Plantation and waited for the British attack. Jackson's troops had built up and fortified a natural levee alongside the Rodriguez Canal. It was from behind this fortified levee that Jackson's troops would defend New Orleans. The British forces were commanded by Maj. Gen. Edward Pakenham. Pakenham's troops had landed a few miles below this location and marched to meet Jackson on the morning of January 8th, 1815.

On paper, Pakenham's plan seems to have been a sound one. The idea was for the British troops to advance forward in three columns. The middle column was the largest and was to march straight forward to engage the Americans. The two outside columns were to arc outwards to the left and right with the goal of going beyond the edges of the American lines and then working their way behind the lines. It was a classic pincer movement where the British hoped to attack the American forces from the front and rear. The British plan fell apart rather quickly when the British neared a large open area leading to the Americans. The Mississippi River was directly to the left of the British. The river took a sharp bend right at that location and came up almost to the British lines. This prevented the left column from arcing outwards. The left column composed of the famed Sutherland Highlanders, the 93rd Regiment of Foot, was forced to march straightforward into the American cannons. The left column was decimated. The right column did not fare much better. While the right column was able to arc outwards to the right, in doing so they found themselves in the middle of a swamp. The fog in the swamp was reported to be so thick that the British could hardly see their hand in front of their face. They became turned around and lost. They soon began, however, hearing gunfire to their left which they assumed to be the Americans. They decided to advance a little further and then make a turn to the left which they hoped would bring them behind the American lines. Unfortunately for the right column, what they took for American gunfire was actually British gunfire. When they made the turn to the left and came out of the swamp they were not behind the American lines. They were between the British and American lines and took fire from both sides. It was not a good day for the right column.

The main column of the British marched directly towards the American lines across an open field with no cover for them. The Americans had laid their long rifles on top of a reinforced embankment and began firing. For the Americans it was basically target practice. The British, in their red uniforms, began falling. At the end of the battle the death toll for British was some 2,000 including General Pakenham and most of his command staff. The death toll for the Americans on that day was under a dozen. It is quite easy to see how such a decisive win could have propelled all the Americans involved into superhero status. They were truly the rock stars of the day. The death toll for the Americans, however, significantly increased following the battle as a result of malaria contracted from being in insect infested swamp water for days while they fortified the levee of the canal. This higher American death toll, however, was often discounted in most historical accounts as it did not portray the same romantic outcome as the death toll on the day of the battle.

Regardless of which account one read, I began to see a growing problem and one simple question for which I could not find an answer. I would walk the entire battlefield and look at the Mississippi River. For the life of me I could not understand, and could find no reason published in any book, as to why General Pakenham landed below the American lines and marched to engage Jackson where he did. All Pakenham would have needed to do was sail right past the American line, sail five more miles, and he would have landed in an almost defenseless New Orleans. The most that Jackson's troops could have done was wave at him as he passed by. He could have taken the city with almost no fight at all. Pakenham was, by no means, an inexperienced general. In all other battles and skirmishes around New Orleans, the British were winning, and soundly. Things did not look well at all for the Americans, at least, not before the morning of the final battle. So, why did Pakenham land where he did and fight where he did? It makes no sense. Clearly the whole story was not being told.

Let's take a look at some of the players on the American side to see what we know, or maybe *believe* that we know. First would have to be Andrew Jackson, the commander of the American forces at the Battle of New Orleans. Jackson was reported to be a 13 or 14-year-old courier for the American army during the war for independence. Reports say that Jackson was captured by the British and beaten thereby accounting for Jackson's strong dislike of the British. It is unknown if this story is true a part of the legend/lore created about Jackson in later years. Jackson was a Freemason and a member of what would become Harmony Lodge No. 1 under the Grand Lodge of Tennessee. Jackson would become Grand Master of the Grand Lodge of Tennessee in 1822 and then elected President of the United States in 1829. It is likely that both of these events were the result of the notoriety and fame of Jackson following the Battle of New Orleans. Another politician and Freemason that played a role in the events was William C.C. Claiborne who was the first governor of Louisiana in 1812. Claiborne was a member of Louisiana Lodge prior to the creation of the Grand Lodge of Louisiana and then became a member of Perfect Union Lodge No. 1. Claiborne's famous feud with the Lafitte brothers might well have set into motion a chain of events that led to the final outcome of the battle. Then we have Jean and Pierre Lafitte, two brothers who were called pirates or buccaneers depending on if one favored or did not favor them. Without question, the Battle of New Orleans could not have achieved the outcome that it did were not for the actions of Jean Lafitte. There is no record of Masonic membership of either of the Lafitte brothers. Then we have Captain Dominique You (sometimes spelled Youx), the commander of Jackson's cannons. You was a member of Charity Lodge No.2 under the Grand Lodge of Louisiana and today has a lodge carrying his name. While it is not proven, You is often said to have been a cannoneer in Napoleon's army, moving to New Orleans at some point prior to the creation of the Grand Lodge in 1812. Another controversial, and sometimes heatedly debated, rumor about You is that he was the elder brother of Jean and Pierre Lafitte. The rumor says that the decision was made to keep You out of the questionable activities of his two younger brothers. The rumor goes on to say that this desire to keep the elder brother legitimate is the reason for the surname change. Regardless of the fact or fiction of this rumor, You was a liaison between the Lafitte brothers and Andrew Jackson.

Andrew Jackson had been given a daunting task by the American government. A large buildup of British ships and troops in the Caribbean islands had been noticed by the Americans. It was felt that an attack on America by the British was forthcoming. It was reasonable that the goal of the attack would be to capture the valuable port of New Orleans. The problem for the Americans was that they had no idea when the attack would take place or where the British would land. Reports said that the landing could be as far east as Mobile or as far west as Lafayette. Jackson based himself in New Orleans but realized that he had nowhere near a suitable troop size to defend such a large area. Another problem for Jackson was that he was extremely low on both gunpowder and flints. He simply did not have enough men to defend the area and even if he did have the men, the gunpowder and flint shortage would render any defense futile. Jackson was not in good shape.

At the same time, William Claiborne was having different problems in New Orleans. Claiborne was shocked by what he felt was the lawlessness of the Creole population in New Orleans. The toleration and even support of the citizens towards the smuggling operations of the Lafitte brothers confused and frustrated Claiborne. His disapproving attitude towards the Creoles made him unpopular in the city. Regardless, Claiborne was determined to clean up the city, and he felt that the first place to start was with the Lafitte brothers. Claiborne ordered wanted posters to be placed all over New Orleans (at that time limited to what is today the French Quarter). The posters offered a $500 reward for anyone who would deliver the Lafitte brothers to Claiborne. The following week a new set of wanted posters were hanging all over the city. These posters offered a $1,000 reward for anyone who could deliver Claiborne to the Lafitte brothers in Barataria Bay. Claiborne was said to be livid. He was outraged by what he considered to be an audacious insult. Claiborne was more determined than ever to capture the Lafittes. It is not certain, however, if the hostile feelings that Claiborne had for the Lafittes was reciprocated. It is possible that the Lafittes were more dismissive of Claiborne and were only poking fun at him for their own amusement. Regardless of how the Lafitte brothers felt about Claiborne, they should have taken more care with him. On a trip into New Orleans, Pierre Lafitte was captured by the authorities and placed into the jail of the Cabildo.[1]

Around the same time as the capture of Pierre Lafitte, visitors arrived at the Lafitte hideout in Barataria Bay.[2] The British had come calling with an offer for Jean Lafitte. They told Lafitte that they knew of his dislike for the authorities and asked for his help. They explained their plan of attacking New Orleans but said that they needed a map in order to navigate the difficult waterways leading into the city. In return for his help, the British offered payment and turning a blind eye to Lafitte's activities in the area. Lafitte is reported to have asked the outcome if he refused the offer. He was told that the British would find their own way into the city, and as they passed Lafitte's base, they would turn their guns on him. Lafitte agreed to the offer.

Completely objective and reliable accounts of Jean Lafitte are difficult to find. A common opinion is that he was a vain man who was skilled at business but strongly disliked being challenged or questioned. The threat following the British offer must not have set well with Lafitte. He was also not at all happy about his brother sitting in the jail of the Cabildo. Lafitte had some past dealings with the Louisiana

Secretary of State and contacted him about the British offer. Lafitte said that he would provide all the information that the British gave him if Claiborne would compensate him and release his brother from jail. Claiborne flatly refused. He said that he did not believe that Lafitte had any information that was of any value and that his brother was going to remain in jail. Claiborne added that soon Jean Lafitte would be joining his brother. Undaunted, Jean Lafitte turned in another direction. He contacted Dominique You. Lafitte made You the same offer that he made to Claiborne, but he added something extra. When You initially contacted Jackson about the offer, Jackson was not impressed. He felt that Lafitte could not be trusted. You assured Jackson that Lafitte's offer was legitimate and then added the "extra" enticement. You told Jackson that Lafitte had a large supply of gun powder and flints that he would include in his offer if Jackson accepted. That tipped the scales for Jackson. He agreed to meet Lafitte and the meeting was reportedly held at what is today The Old Absinthe House on Bourbon Street. The building was then Lafitte's importing firm (smugglings operation), in the heart of the city's French Quarter. Jackson agreed to the offer and then went to see Claiborne about the release of Pierre Lafitte.

The meeting between Andrew Jackson and William Claiborne concerning the release of Pierre Lafitte is a matter of pure speculation as to exactly what was said between the two. All that is known for certain is that Jackson asked for the release of Lafitte and Claiborne refused. Given the fiery temper of both men, it can be assumed that some sharp words were exchanged, but the outcome was final. Claiborne would not release Pierre Lafitte. Jackson had no authority to order the release of Lafitte as he was being held on state charges. So, what was Jackson going to do? He needed the powder and flits in order to have any hope of success against the British. He had also already given his agreement to Jean Lafitte's offer. Claiborne had placed Jackson in an extremely difficult position.

The problem for Jackson concerning Pierre Lafitte, however, seems to have solved itself several days later. According to the newspapers of the day, Lafitte "escaped" from the jail of the Cabildo. No details have ever been published as to *how* this "escape" was accomplished. All that we know for certain is that Pierre Lafitte escaped, he rejoined his brother in Barataria Bay, and Jackson received the information about the British attack along with all the gun powder and flints that he needed. So, without any evidence to support this statement, I'm going to venture a guess that Pierre Lafitte had some help in his escape. I'm going to suggest that the jailer, who was also a Mason, went to Lafitte's jail cell, unlocked the cell door and told him something along the lines of, "Get out of here, your friends are waiting for you outside." Nothing else makes sense. The Cabildo was not a place from which people escaped. Anyone who has seen the jail of the Cabildo realizes why no one had escaped prior to this event. Without question, Jackson would not have received the information on the British, the gun powder, or the flints if Pierre Lafitte remained in jail. Where history remains silent, logic must fill in the gaps.

Andrew Jackson was now in far better position than he was prior to his meeting with Jean Lafitte. But problems still remained. He knew that the attack was going to come directly to New Orleans, but he did not know exactly which route into the city the British would take. Jackson sent word to all the troops stationed along the Gulf Coast to return immediately to New Orleans. It was time for Jackson to devise a plan to defend the city. Jackson and his military command are often said to have met at Maspero's Coffee House on Chartrer's Street (but it cannot be proven). The details of the meeting are as sketchy as the location.

Shortly before Christmas of 1814, the British warships were at the mouth of the Mississippi River. Jackson had begun his defense of New Orleans by building up the levee at the Rodriguez Canal. A number of skirmishes with the British took place, mostly on the west bank of the

Mississippi. None of these battles ended well for the Americans. It was at this time that a single American schooner, the *USS Carolina*, under the command of J. D. Henley (rumored, but never proven to be a Freemason) sailed out to engage the British. The *Carolina* fired on the British warships. Return fire from the British quickly set the *Carolina* on fire and the bulk of the crew, including Henley, were captured. The *Carolina* exploded and sank. This is the thumbnail, generally accepted history of the events just prior to the final Battle of New Orleans. When we stop and consider the events, serious questions of logic arise that are unanswered in the historical accounts.

Why were the American forces so unsuccessful against the British in all of the engagements around New Orleans except the final battle? Why would a woefully under-gunned single schooner sail out to engage a fleet of British warships? Was Henley suicidal? Why did Jackson select the Rodriguez Canal as the location to place all of his troops to defend New Orleans? And finally, why in the world did Pakenham land his ships just below the Rodriguez Canal and march right into the American defenses when he could have landed literally anywhere else and had little to no resistance in capturing New Orleans? These questions are simply not answered in the historical accounts.

Let's look at the situation through the eyes of a historian who must use logic and supposition to fill in the holes where evidence does not exist. To start with, the final battle at the Rodriguez Canal in what is now the town of Chalmette was such a decisive American victory that it seems to have overshadowed everything else about the events. The Americans did not see themselves as lucky to have won, but as an invincible force that could not possibly lose regardless of the opponent. Jackson, You and the Lafitte brothers became super stars with songs, stories and legends built around them. But the serious questions surrounding the events must be answered and thin, unsupported rumors must be looked at a bit harder. For example, J.D. Henley's actions with the *Carolina* are astonishing. What did he hope to gain? Why would any responsible commander take a ship that he knew full well had no chance at all of inflicting any serious damage into such an attack? He must have known the only logical outcome. Yet, he risked the lives of all his men and the ship as well for nothing at all. Or is that true? There is a completely unproven rumor that has floated around for many years. It is completely discounted as it may take something away from the invincible status of the American army. Let's look at it.

Andrew Jackson held a planning meeting of his military commanders. It can be logically assumed that Henley was present. The rumor exists that Jackson knew the danger facing New Orleans and that the most defendable route into New Orleans was through the Rodriguez Canal. Jackson knew that the location was perfect. With the river on one side and a swamp on the other, the British would be forced into a bottle neck and by necessity, march across an open field with zero cover. The American troops, however, would be protected by a reinforced levee. Jackson knew that this was his choice for the battle, but how could he get the British to come to his party? He sought to devise a plan where the British would want to use this route for their attack on New Orleans. It is here that Henley is said to have presented an interesting suggestion. Henley would take the *Carolina* out and attack the British warships. The British would quickly overpower the *Carolina* and capture the crew. As was their normal practice, they would question the captain of the ship. One of the certain questions would be about the American defenses around New Orleans. Henley would then do something completely unthinkable and unbelievable for an officer and a gentleman of that time. He would lie. He would tell the British that the Americans were long expecting an attack on New Orleans and the city was very heavily defended all around the city, except for one route. He would then hesitate and feign giving more information. Upon pressure, Henley would tell the British that the only lightly defended route into New Orleans was through the Chalmette Plantation across the Rodriguez Canal. Instead of telling the British of the only weak link in the American defenses, he told them the very route of the only defended one.

Of course, Jackson would have no way of knowing if the British would actually fall for this ruse or not. But, what else could he do? He had one shot, and this seemed to be the very best idea to get the British where he wanted them. He had only one back up plan. If the British did sail right past the American lines, Jackson had a small group of men stationed all around the city with only one job — burn the city to the ground. He was not going to allow the British to capture New Orleans.

Is any of this provable fact? Much of it is not. This paper should be read as a logical examination of things unproven and even undocumented in Louisiana history. It is a theory based on a basic understanding of the events. But, as we all know, the British did land below the Rodriguez Canal and the outcome of the battle went down as one of the greatest wins for the American army. These are facts.

By the way, I somewhat skimmed over one part of this story. I mentioned that the jailer guarding Pierre Lafitte in the Cabildo was a Mason. That's not conjecture. That's fact. He was the one who seems to have put doing what was necessary for the "greater good" ahead of what was the technical law. He was a man who was concerned with doing what was right, not easy or safe. In fact, if it were not for him, we can look at the whole of the Battle of New Orleans with a quite different ending. I cannot reasonably see any of the events that would happen actually happen if Pierre Lafitte had not "escaped." The "escape" of Pierre Lafitte allowed everything else to happen. I believe that the forgotten hero of the Battle of New Orleans was that jailer. The jailer was not only a Mason but would end up serving as Grand Master of the Grand Lodge of Louisiana as well as play a rather significant role in Texas Freemasonry. The young jailer's name: John Henry Holland. Most Worshipful Brother Holland had a long history of doing what was *right* rather than what was popular, advantageous to him personally, or technically *proper*. He realized that sometimes we need to step up and get the things done that we all know needs to be done. He was a man of action. He was the true definition of a Masonic leader. I believe it is most fitting that a Mason of such honor, integrity, and courage would be the one to issue the warrant for the first lodge in Texas.

Notes:

1. In the days of the Spanish rule of Louisiana, the Cabildo was the Spanish city hall of New Orleans. It today serves as a Louisiana State Museum. The Cabilo is next to the St. Louis Cathedral across from Jackson Square.
2. Barataria Bay is located in the Gulf of Mexico near southeastern Louisiana close to Grand Isle and Grand Terre.

Discovering the Present Day
Supreme Council of Louisiana
By Michael R. Poll

I joined Freemasonry in New Orleans in 1975. Like most all who join, my actual knowledge of Masonry at that time was expectedly limited and superficial. I had several family members who were Masons, but I really only knew the very basics of the nature of Freemasonry and certainly not much in the area of Masonic history. Several years later, I joined the *Valley of New Orleans*. I knew even less about the Scottish Rite. I did, however, know one thing very clearly — I was impressed to no end with the Masonic philosophy and ritual, especially concerning the Scottish Rite.

While I was deeply impressed with the Scottish Rite, there was another aspect of which I became quickly aware. The *Valley of New Orleans* was, for lack of a better term, an emotional place. Laughter in the valley could be quick, deep and genuine. But at the same time, there was a cloud of hurt and anger that seemed to always be present and could surface at almost any time. I didn't understand why at the time, but the emotion in the valley was tangible.

My craft lodge had two members who were 33rds in the *New Orleans Valley*. In itself, that is not such an unusual accomplishment as many lodges can boast of members who hold the 33rd degree. What was, however, very unusual about these members was the title in the Scottish Rite that they both held. They were both Past Grand Masters of Kadosh of the *Grand Consistory of Louisiana*. That's a title you don't hear every day. You see, from 1811[1] until 1973 (just several years before I joined), the *Valley of New Orleans* was the *Grand Consistory of Louisiana*. The presiding officer of the Grand Consistory was the Grand Master of Kadosh. In 1973, Sovereign Grand Commander Henry Clausen downgraded the *Grand Consistory of Louisiana* (the last grand consistory under the *Southern Jurisdiction*) into a statutory consistory of the *Valley of New Orleans*.[2] This action of abolishing the *Grand Consistory* can explain much (but not all) of the bad feelings in the valley at the time of my joining. There was a general feeling that much was being, and had been, unfairly taken from New Orleans.

Whenever I speak about this subject, the question often arises, "What is a grand consistory?" To give you a little background, a grand consistory is a Scottish Rite body subordinate to a supreme council, but superior to lodges of perfection or other Scottish Rite bodies. In the grand lodge system, you might think of a grand consistory as something along the lines of a provincial grand lodge. Its job was to provide local supervision to bodies under the jurisdiction of the supreme council, but at a considerable distance from the council itself.[3] The collective voice and vote of a grand consistory carried the same authority as a Sovereign Grand Inspector General. The *Valley of New Orleans*, and that includes its time as the *Grand Consistory of Louisiana*, is the oldest continually active high-grade body of Ancient and Accepted Scottish Rite Masonry in North or South America.

Another body that I learned about soon after joining the *Valley of New Orleans* was a body identified to me as the *"New Orleans Supreme Council."* Wow, what a collection of stories I learned about this body! And, what an exercise in contradiction. After reading a few of the books and documents and listening to members, I had no idea in the world who or what to believe concerning this body. When I listened to the stories told by some of the then senior members of the valley, I learned of a near mythical body akin to a Shangri-La or Camelot where everything was done correctly, everyone was wise & kind and everyone content. But then, the stories continued, others became jealous of this utopian paradise. Outsiders wished the New Orleans Scottish Rite harm and sought all that they possessed. The New Orleans Scottish Rite Masons were tricked, lied to and destroyed just so that everything good about them could be taken away.

Interestingly enough, there was another side to the coin and a *very* different story. When I read any of the old Scottish Rite history books, and that included the grand-daddy of all Louisiana Masonic history books, *Outline of the Rise and Progress of Freemasonry in Louisiana*, a completely different tale was told. In these accounts, it was the *New Orleans Supreme Council* who were the bad guys. It was not just a body of Masons who held a different view of Masonry, nor was it simply an irregular body. The *New Orleans Supreme Council* was a collection of morally corrupt gangsters. They were portrayed as near monsters who would steal the Masonic souls of the naive and foolish, all so that they could practice their perverted Scottish Rite abomination.

I couldn't believe what I was reading and hearing. This was not just a little difference of opinion; the stories were complete spectrum opposites. The "other guys" were not just wrong, but pure evil! I was absolutely fascinated. I also found it amazing that both sides offered their arguments with an outrageous lack of evidence, but always with extreme emotion. The *only* thing that both sides agreed upon was that this supreme council died off in the late 1800's.

There was no question in my mind - I *had* to do my own research into this astonishing historical puzzle. I just needed a place to start.

My first goal was to collect and study as many of the old Masonic and Scottish Rite history books as I could find. Most were long out of print. I visited used bookstores and Masonic, public and university libraries. When I could not buy a book, I would find one in a library or elsewhere and photocopy it. I spent months pouring over these books. The next step was to try and locate as many of the documents mentioned in the books as possible. I contacted the then Grand Secretary of the *Grand Lodge of Louisiana*, RW Brother Jack Crouch and the then Sovereign Grand Inspector General in Louisiana, Ill Brother D. Walter Jessen and asked both for letters of introduction. Both kindly gave me wonderful letters which allowed me to contact grand lodges and supreme councils with questions and requests of aid in my search.

As my search for documents continued, I began to realize that it was necessary for me to travel to various locations and do "boots on the ground" research (the internet did not exist in those days). I visited both the *Southern Jurisdiction* and *Northern Masonic Jurisdiction* in my quest. Both supreme council visits brought me valuable documents from which I gained insight, but my trip to the *Southern Jurisdiction* brought much more.

I was in communication with Dr. John Boettcher, the then Editor of the *Scottish Rite Journal* for some time. The communications normally concerned things I had written and were published in both the *Scottish Rite Journal* and its earlier incarnation, *The New Age*. I had also worked on several research projects with the then Librarian of the House of the Temple, Mrs. Inge Baum. I contacted Dr. Boettcher and made plans for a visit. I explained that I was looking for any documents relating to early Scottish Rite Masonry in Louisiana and the troubled times of the "Scottish Rite war" before and after the *Concordat of 1855*.[4]

Upon arriving at the *House of the Temple*, I was greeted by Dr. Boettcher and given a tour of the building. It was beautiful. As we walked into the library, I was impressed with the large collection of books, but really, I expected nothing less. We were greeted by a slight, elderly lady who was smiling from ear to ear; it was Mrs. Baum. After a few friendly words, she led me to a long, beautiful table that took up a large portion of the room. The table had a good many chairs on both sides and chairs at the head and foot. I noticed a large stack of papers right to the side of the head of the table. This is where Mrs. Baum was leading me. She pointed at the papers and told me that this was the collection of Louisiana documents that I had requested. She had an odd smile and look in her eyes. She then asked me if I knew why she had placed the documents in that particular spot on the table. I told her that I had no idea. She then said with a large smile that this was the location where the last person who requested Louisiana documents always sat when he studied them. She then asked me if I knew of whom she was speaking. I told her that I did not. With an even larger smile she said, "Mr. Clausen." With a bit of surprise, I asked her if she meant Past Sovereign Grand Commander Henry Clausen. She said yes and that he came to the library at least several times a week, sat in that very spot and studied anything and everything he could find concerning the Louisiana Scottish Rite and Louisiana Masonry. I was more than a little surprised and filed that information away for later consideration.

On the same trip, I planned on visiting the *Grand Lodge of the District of Columbia*. I had communicated a number of times with the then Grand Secretary, MWBro Stewart Miner and became friendly with him. He was very interested in Masonic research and provided me with great assistance in researching the archives of his grand lodge. During my visit, MWBro Miner told me that he wanted me to meet several young researchers with whom he had become acquainted over the last few years. He said one, in particular, had also shown great interest in researching the early history of the Scottish Rite. He was a Texas Mason by the name of Arturo de Hoyos. Over the next few years, Art and I would become good friends and make trips to the House of the Temple together in search of Scottish Rite documents. We also spent countless hours on the phone discussing the "lost history" of the Scottish Rite. Bro. de Hoyos shared my interest in the enigma of the *New Orleans Supreme Council*. It was an amazing academic, Masonic detective mystery.

As I began to delve deeper into the books and documents concerning the troubled Scottish Rite times of the mid 1800's and the heartbreaking war that turned Brother against Brother, an extraordinarily depressing picture started emerging. The language in the books, from both sides, was akin to spitting acid. It didn't matter if it were James Foulhouze, Albert Pike or whoever was writing, it was so, so very harsh. When I would stop and realize that these were *Masons* speaking to, and about, other Masons, I felt physically ill. I had never read anything that reached this level of near hatred. Every possible insult, attack and nastiness was levied against "the other guys" simply because they existed. No one would give an inch. Looking from the outside in, I could begin to see that neither side was completely right nor completely wrong. The only thing that both sides shared was that *neither* were acting very Masonic. The heart of the problem seemed to be ego. Neither side could admit that they could be in *any way* wrong or the other in *any way* right. They both sacrificed Masonry for pride. It was truly the saddest collection of documents I had ever read. All they had to do was put their hand out and welcome the other. The fact that they were both living in glass houses and both insistent on throwing rocks seemed to escape them. Truly, there were no winners in that war.

Some months later, on a visit to the *Grand Lodge of Louisiana*, I was asked by the Grand Secretary if I could take over communicating with someone who I was told was a "French Brother living in Germany." I was told that the brother had shown great interest in the early history of Louisiana Masonry but was asking questions that no one in the Grand Lodge office could answer. I was shown the last letter the brother wrote. I recognized the name immediately. It was WBrother Alain Bernheim.

Over the next few months and years, Bro. Bernheim and I became good friends. We would write each other regularly (starting with postal mail, then fax, and then e-mail) sharing information on Masonic research with special attention to the early history of Louisiana Freemasonry and its Scottish Rite. In one mail to Bro Bernheim, I wrote on how I felt it was such a shame that a body that seemed to be so very regular and Masonic in nature as the *New Orleans Supreme Council* could cease to exist. I lamented on the loss of this historic and significant body. He wrote me back a very short e-mail. He said that he only had two questions for me. The first was why did I continually call that body the

2020 Transactions of the Louisiana Lodge of Research

"*New Orleans Supreme Council*" when their correct name is "*The Supreme Council of Louisiana*"? The second question was why did I continually say that they no longer existed?

I was stunned. As to the first question, I called them that because that was the name that I had always heard them called in New Orleans. I knew their official name but used the common term that I had always heard used. As to the second astonishing question, I told Bro. Bernehim that I assumed that they no longer existed because I have never heard or read a single word to the contrary. I had never seen a scrap of evidence to suggest that they still existed. He wrote me back saying that I am in New Orleans and he is halfway around the world. He said that if I am so sure of their non-existence, then the accounts he learned of must be incorrect.

I remember sitting in the chair at my desk thinking about my exchange with Bro. Bernheim. How ridiculous. I had been a Mason by that time for some 20 years in New Orleans. Not once did I *ever* hear anything of the supreme council still existing. But, what a resounding kick in the pants it would be if they did exist. As I was sitting there, I looked over at the telephone book on my desk. I stared at it for a time and then laughed to myself. It simply could not be possible that they were listed in the phone book. That was too easy. I could no longer help myself, I had to look. I picked up the phone book and flipped through the pages.

I cannot tell you exactly how I felt next. I imagine that the best way to describe it was the old image of someone falling out of their chair in shock. There in the phone book, as big as life was listed, "*The Supreme Council of Louisiana.*" What in the world was going on? Was I in an episode of *The Twilight Zone*? I just sat there for a little while totally bewildered. Then I did the only thing I could think of doing. I picked up the phone and called the number listed. They answered the phone, "*Supreme Council of Louisiana.*" I had no idea what to say. Finally, I said that I had a question to ask. I asked if they were the same supreme council that was created in 1839. The voice on the phone came back with,

"Yes, we are." I thanked him and hung up. What in the world was going on? I had by then spent many years digging into the early history of a body which I *thought* had ceased to exist in the late 1800's. Was I now to believe that they still exist? How stupid could I be? But, in my defense, not *once* did I *ever* see, hear or read *anything* to suggest that they still existed. And, really, what proof did I have that they did still exist? Anyone can list a phone under whatever name they like. That's no proof at all. So, I grabbed my keys, went out to the car and drove to the address given in the phone book.

As I drove up to the building, I recognized it immediately. I had passed by it many times over the years, noticed the signs, but never paid much of any attention to it. I had always assumed that it was some fly-by-night Masonic self-creation. I parked the car and went inside. There were several African-American men inside and one introduced himself as the Secretary-General. He then introduced me to the Sovereign Grand Commander, Philip Washington, Sr. I introduced myself and told them that I had been researching the early history of the AASR and Freemasonry in Louisiana. I felt a bit uncomfortable as I had no idea if this could possibly be the real deal or if they had simply found some old documents or records and self-created a body with an old name. In other words, I didn't know if they were frauds or not.

We talked just a little and most of it was superficial. I then asked if they had a list of their Sovereign Grand Commanders from the time of their creation. The secretary said that he thought he had something like that around. He looked through his desk and pulled out a piece of paper. He made a photocopy of it and gave me the copy. I thanked them all and left.

When I got home, I looked at the paper I was given (See: Appendix A & B). It started off with a list of names that I knew well. But then, following Eugene Chassignac, began a long list of names that I had never seen before. At that time, I noticed something that gave me reason to believe that the body I had just visited was, indeed, a self-created, fraudulent body. Following Eugene Chassignac were 19 names listed as Sovereign Grand Commanders. 17 of the names were printed with the last two (Joseph Williams, 1987 and Philip Washington, Sr., 1993) handwritten onto the list. The last printed name was George Longe, showing that he was elected Sovereign Grand Commander in 1938. That's almost 50 years between the election of George Longe and Joseph Williams. Prior to George Longe, most of the Sovereign Grand Commanders served only a few years. I had no idea how long George Longe served, but it seemed likely to me that *maybe* he served until sometime around WWII and then the council died off to be recreated in 1987 by Joseph Williams.

What interested me most, at the time, were the 17 printed names (some serving more than once) that followed Eugene Chassignac. If these names were proven to actually be Sovereign Grand Commanders of the *Supreme Council of Louisiana*, then it would mean that the council existed far longer than had previously been believed. I wanted to find a way to check out these names and any possible association with the council. I went to the public library.

The *New Orleans Public Library* had provided me with a great deal of help in the past. Their main library had a microfilm section with most all of the old newspapers published in New Orleans in the 1800's. My idea was to look up the death notices in the old papers for each of the names listed and to see if I could find anything of interest. To my amazement, for each and every name I searched I found a death notice published in the newspaper by the *Supreme Council of Louisiana*. The notices were announcing the death of their Sovereign Grand Commander. Every single name was accounted for and each carried such a death notice from the council. It seemed that the *Supreme Council of Louisiana* had existed far longer than had been known. I realized that this was a major discovery. How they could have existed all this time with no record of their existence was a question I put aside for a later time. I then came to the name of George Longe. As I began the search for his death notice I realized that, with this information, I would likely find the actual date of the death of the *Supreme Council of Louisiana*.

Earlier, I mentioned a discovery which was so surprising to me that I almost fell out of my chair. Well, that was when I was in the privacy of my home sitting at my desk. For the same thing to happen to me in a public library was considerably more embarrassing. I found the death notice of George Longe. Like the others, it carried a notice from the *Supreme Council of Louisiana*. But George Longe didn't die until late 1985. My mind was whirling. If the council died in the 30's, 40's or 50's, then how could it announce his death in 1985?[5] Does this mean that George Longe served as Sovereign Grand Commander for almost 50 years? Does this mean that the body I visited is *actually* the very same supreme council that I learned about when I joined Masonry?

There were just too many questions for me to deal with at that time. I needed a bit of time to process everything and think about the information in a logical and structured manner. I decided to take some time off and let things sink in and only then formulate my next steps. But sometimes things don't go as we plan.

In boxing there is something known as a one-two punch. The first part of that punch came at the library with the discovery concerning George Longe. The second part of the punch came the very next day. I went early to the *University of New Orleans* to pick up a French to English translation of an old Masonic document that I had found some time back. I was able to make my way though many of the old French writings, but when I suspected something was important, I would call on a friend of mine who was a French Professor at the university. I spoke to him of some of the discoveries. He was not a Mason, but very interested. He told me that I really should go to the history department and speak with one of the instructors there. She had recently received her PhD and a good part of her dissertation was on, of all things, early Louisiana Freemasonry, especially Scottish Rite Freemasonry in New Orleans. I walked over to the history department and met Dr. Caryn Cossé Bell.[6] We talked a while, and I gave her a few names of key figures in my research. She knew them all. I then asked her if she knew of George Longe. She said that she knew of him well and asked if I visited "his collection" at Tulane University. I had not and had no idea of what she was speaking. Dr. Bell gave me directions to the building to find the collection and I was off like a shot.

When I arrived at Tulane, I went to find the collection.[7] If I tried to explain how I felt when I saw what was in that collection, I imagine the best way that I can describe it is to think of that little boy upon first arriving in Willy Wonka's candy factory. I was overwhelmed. It was not just a large collection of Scottish Rite documents; it was a large collection of extremely important Scottish Rite documents. To give just one example, within that collection I found what is today known as The Bonseigneur Rituals.[8] It is a collection of 18th century New Orleans Ecossais Masonic Rituals. I sent copy of these rituals to Alain Bernheim upon finding them for dating. I also sent a copy to Gerald Prinsen of the Latomia Foundation in the Netherlands for publication. The rituals are a hand-written copy of a much older collection of rituals. The copy is dated as being made about 1785 to the early 1790's and some of the rituals look to date prior to 1750. Even with this aside, it is very possibly the lost rituals of the Grand Lodge of Louisiana, being worked by the Grand Lodge and the 5 French speaking lodges that created it. This significant find was made in their collection. To this day, I have not completely explored all of the collection.

The first thing that I did upon entering the collection was to pull out that list of Sovereign Grand Commanders and search for each of them in the collection. I was able to find letters, documents, diplomas and other official records for each of them signing as the Sovereign Grand Commander of the *Supreme Council of Louisiana*. Yep, George Longe served as Sovereign Grand Commander for almost 50 years! There was now no doubt, the body known today as the Supreme Council of Louisiana is the very same body from the 1800's. But, apart from a foot note, what does it mean? Then, years later, came 2011.

It was the 200th anniversary of the creation of the Grand Consistory of Louisiana — the one valley of high grade Ancient and Accepted Scottish Rite Freemasonry that continued to exist when all others in the United States slumbered. A foresighted Scottish Rite Honorary Sovereign Grand Inspector General and Past Grand Master of the Grand Lodge of Louisiana, Clayton J. Borne, III, felt that a celebration was in order. He obtained permission and organized a Scottish Rite symposium where the Scottish Rite could be celebrated and studied by means of public lectures on the Scottish Rite.

On June 1st to 4th, 2011, for the first time in history, representatives of the *Supreme Council, Southern Jurisdiction, USA*; the *Supreme Council of Louisiana* and the *Grand Lodge of Louisiana* joined together with the representatives of other supreme councils and Grand Lodges to meet at the Royal Sonesta Hotel on Royal Street in New Orleans ... and peace and harmony prevailed. The symposium location was just steps away from where Albert Mackey met with James Foulhouze in Mackey's failed attempt to have Foulhouze join the *Southern Jurisdiction*.[9] There was no ritual, no "secrets" exchanged, no compromising situations. It was a public gathering that was, in this writer's experience, the most truly Masonic gathering I have ever attended. It was beautiful.

Through knowledge, we now have an opportunity. We will own the choices we make. But what will we do? Continue a pointless "war," continue a policy of "hidden in plain sight" or respect others who do the true work of the Scottish Rite? Do we battle against ourselves or against ignorance?

The beauty of the future is that it is an open book. Upon it we can write whatever path we choose. We now know far more about this aspect of our Scottish Rite history than we knew not too many years ago. And, with that knowledge we can do whatever we like. The future of the Scottish Rite is up to us. I truly hope that we can put all the pain, misinformation, ego, and nonsense aside and once again become what the creators of Louisiana Freemasonry saw as Freemasonry.

Notes:

1. The earliest known appearance of the *Grand Consistory of Louisiana* was in New Orleans in 1811. There are unfortunately, no known surviving minutes or documents from this body. Most all of the information that has been collected concerning the 1811 Grand Consistory is recorded in a few secondary sources. James Scot gives us, in his 1873 *Outline of the Rise and Progress of Freemasonry in Louisiana*, a piece of information concerning this body by reproducing a communication dated 20 April 1811 from the *Sov. Grand Consistory of Princes of the Royal Secret of Louisiana* to *Etoile Polaire Lodge*. The communication seeks to establish relations between the *Grand Consistory* and *Etoile Polaire Lodge* and is issued under the name of "Des Bois, Grand Secretary." (See: James Scot, *Outline of the Rise and Progress of Freemasonry in Louisiana* 1873 [New Orleans, LA: Cornerstone Book Publishers, reprint 2008.] pp. 21-22). Also, in his 1882 "Official Bulletin V," Albert Pike tells us that on March 28, 1811 the *Grand Consistory of Louisiana* was granted a charter by Louis Jean Lusson and Jean Baptiste Modeste Lefebvre, both SGIG's of the *Supreme Council of Kingston, Jamaica*. Pike also tells us that on Sunday, April 7, 1811 at 5 p.m., in the hall of *Perfect Union Lodge*, the *Grand Consistory* held its first meeting. The meeting was attended by many of the "founding fathers" of Louisiana Freemasonry, who were Members of this *Grand Consistory*. (See: Albert Pike, *Official Bulletin of the Supreme Council of the 33rd Degree for the Southern Jurisdiction of the United States*. Washington, D.C. 1882). For many years 1813 was given as the creation date (incorrectly) for the *Grand Consistory of Louisiana*. This was the year that the *Grand Consistory* passed under the jurisdiction of the Cerneau *Sovereign Grand Consistory* (supreme council) in New York. The Cerneau system used different names for some of their bodies and this is why from 1813 to the early 1830's the surviving Minutes of the *Grand Consistory of Louisiana* show that it was known as the *Grand COUNCIL of Louisiana*. It was

still a body of the 32nd degree but used a different name. So strong was the attachment to Cerneau by the Louisiana Masons that they seem to have "forgotten" the time of their existence before Cerneau. (*Minutes Book of the Grand Consistory of Louisiana* [1822-1846]). Located in the *New Orleans Scottish Rite Bodies.* New Orleans, Louisiana.) See also: Michael R. Poll, "The Early Years of the Grand Consistory of Louisiana (1811-1815)." *Heredom Vol. 8,* (Washington, D.C., The Scottish Rite Research Society, 1999-2000) pp. 39-53., Auturo de Hoyos, "The Early Years of the Grand Consistory of Louisiana (1811-1815) - A Rejoinder" & Michael R. Poll, "A Few 'Rejoinder' Comments." Both: *Heredom Vol. 9,* (Washington, D.C., The Scottish Rite Research Society, 2001) pp. 69-110.

2. "For multiple reasons, I directed that the Grand Consistory of Louisiana be converted into a statutory consistory of the Valley of New Orleans. I outlined the required procedure, and our Grand Secretary General processed the necessary papers. Grand Consistories were inaugurated when communications over long distances were difficult. Later they were found to be impediment to effective administration so became outmoded. All except Louisiana had been converted into statutory consistories. There is no longer any sanction under our Statues for a Grand Consistory." -Henry C. Clausen, 33°, Sovereign Grand Commander. See: *Transactions of the Supreme Council, 33° for the Southern Jurisdiction, USA* (Washington, D.C, Supreme Council, 33° for the Southern Jurisdiction, USA, 1973) p. 46

3. See: Albert Mackey, *An Encyclopedia of Freemasonry* (New York, NY, The Masonic History company, 1925), p. 305

4. See: Ray Baker Harris, James D. Carter, *History of the Supreme Council, 33° Southern Jurisdiction, USA (1801-1861)* (Washington, D.C.: The Supreme Council, 33° 1964) This Scottish Rite "war" centered itself on the reawakened "Charleston Supreme Council" (*Supreme Council, Southern Jurisdiction, USA*) and the "New Orleans Supreme Council" (*Supreme Council of Louisiana*). The two councils argued over regularity with half of the *New Orleans Council* signing a concordat in 1855 to pass under the jurisdiction of the *Charleston Council* and half refusing to participate. In 1856, the half of the *New Orleans Council* which refused to sign the concordat, announced that the action of signing the Charleston concordat was illegal and that the *New Orleans Council* continued to exist. In 1857, the powerful Past Sovereign Grand Commander, attorney and judge, James Foulhouze returned as Sovereign Grand Commander of the

New Orleans Council. The *Charleston Council* answered with the young attorney, Albert Pike, being elected Sovereign Grand Commander in 1859 (the first *election* of a Grand Commander in the *Charleston Council's* history). The two went toe to toe in an epic battle equaling the Charleston/Cerneau battle some years earlier. See also: James Foulhouze, *Historical Inquiry into the Origins of the Ancient and Accepted Scottish Rite,* 1858, (New Orleans, LA: Cornerstone Book Publishers, reprint 2012).

5. It did not escape me that George Longe's death was in 1985, but the next Sovereign Grand Commander was not elected until 1987. I learned later that Longe was suffering from dementia for a number of years prior to his death. During this time, the Lt. Grand Commander assumed the day to day duties of the Grand Commander and continued them until time of the 1987 election. It seems that the council was in something of shock as Longe had served in office for so very long and had been such a massive and successful figure in the council, that there was uncertainty as how to carry on after his death. The only other time which seemed to have brought such sock to a supreme council was in the Southern Jurisdiction following the death of Albert Pike.

6. Dr. Bell's doctoral dissertation was first published (hardback) by the Louisiana State University Press in 1996. In 2004, it was released in paperback as, *Revolution, Romanticism, and the Afro-Creole Protest Tradition in Louisiana, 1718-1868* (Baton Rouge, LA Louisiana State University Press, 2004).

7. The George Longe Collection is located in *The Amistad Research Center* at Tulane University in New Orleans, LA. On-line, the collection can be found at: http://www.amistadresearchcenter.org.

8. *The Bonseigneur Rituals,* (The Netherlands, The Latomia Foundation, 1996. Republished in the USA by Cornerstone Book Publishers, New Orleans, LA, 2008)

9. Michael R. Poll, "James Fouhouze: Sovereign Grand Commander of the Supreme Council of Louisiana" *Heredom Vol. 6,* (Washington, D.C., The Scottish Rite Research Society, 1997) pp. 64-69.

www.ingramcontent.com/pod-product-compliance
Lightning Source LLC
Chambersburg PA
CBHW021104090426
42738CB00006B/495